教育部、国家语委重大文化工程

 "中华思想文化术语传播工程"成果

国家社科基金重大项目

 "中国核心术语国际影响力研究"（项目号：21&ZD158）成果

北京市法学会市级法学研究青年课题

 "北京市红色法治文化资源整理与保护研究"

 （立项编号：BLS（2022）C007）成果

中华思想文化术语传播工程

Key Concepts in
Chinese Thought and Culture

崔蕴华 李驰 编著
田力男 王敏 译

中国传统法治文化术语

汉英对照

Key Concepts in Traditional Chinese Rule of Law Culture
(Chinese-English)

外语教学与研究出版社
FOREIGN LANGUAGE TEACHING AND RESEARCH PRESS
北京 BEIJING

图书在版编目 (CIP) 数据

中国传统法治文化术语：汉英对照 / 崔蕴华，李驰编著；田力男，王敏译. —— 北京：外语教学与研究出版社，2022.10（2023.7 重印）
 ISBN 978-7-5213-4050-1

Ⅰ. ①中… Ⅱ. ①崔… ②李… ③田… ④王… Ⅲ. ①社会主义法治－文化研究－名词术语－汉、英 Ⅳ. ①D920.0-61

中国版本图书馆 CIP 数据核字 (2022) 第 197569 号

出版人	王　芳
责任编辑	钱垂君
责任校对	刘　佳
封面设计	李　高
版式设计	XXL Studio
出版发行	外语教学与研究出版社
社　　址	北京市西三环北路 19 号（100089）
网　　址	https://www.fltrp.com
印　　刷	北京捷迅佳彩印刷有限公司
开　　本	710×1000　1/16
印　　张	14
版　　次	2022 年 11 月第 1 版　2023 年 7 月第 2 次印刷
书　　号	ISBN 978-7-5213-4050-1
定　　价	58.00 元

如有图书采购需求，图书内容或印刷装订等问题，侵权、盗版书籍等线索，请拨打以下电话或关注官方服务号：
客服电话：400 898 7008
官方服务号：微信搜索并关注公众号"外研社官方服务号"
外研社购书网址：https://fltrp.tmall.com

物料号：340500001

本书编委会

| 张永然 | 崔蕴华 | 姜晓敏 |
| 李　驰 | 王怡然 | 穆云航 |

The Editorial Board

| Zhang Yongran | Cui Yunhua | Jiang Xiaomin |
| Li Chi | Wang Yiran | Mu Yunhang |

编写说明

《中国传统法治文化术语》是以习近平法治思想为指引，以中国特色社会主义法治理论为依据，挑选传统法治文化领域的重要术语加以解读和呈现的成果。

一、主要内容

《中国传统法治文化术语》由思想理念、法律制度和法律文化三个部分组成：第一部分收录体现法治形成与发展中的标志性观点、理念、理论等精神文明的术语；第二部分收录体现法治形成与发展中的典型机制、体制、体系等制度文明的术语；第三部分收录体现影响法治文化形成与发展的术语，包括标志、符号、器物、设施等。

二、选取原则

《中国传统法治文化术语》挑选的是能够反映中国传统法治文化的词汇或短语，共107条，遴选时依照以下三大原则：其一，典型性，即术语在日常实践中已被广泛使用且有较高辨识度。其二，历史性，即术语有较为深厚的历史积淀或实践积累。其三，专业性，即术语能够在一定程度上反映现代法学精神。

三、编写标准

术语编写标准主要有以下五点：其一，表述简洁。在保证专业性的前提下，用简单直观的语言表达其内涵。其二，内涵明确。描述力求准确、到位，内容没有歧义，没有重大理论争议。其三，价值积极。内容积极向上，符合弘扬社会主义核心价值观的要求。其四，时代特征。内涵解读配合2035年建成法治国家、法治政府和法治社会的实际需要。其五，易于传播。编写内容和形式符合人们的阅读习惯，以提高术语的可接受度。

四、呈现形式

术语以条目汇编的形式呈现，内容包括术语名称、理论内涵（概念、起源、发展、价值、意义等）、引例、英译文。

本书的术语具有短小精悍、内涵丰富的特点，对传统法治文化术语的传播有助于解决目前普法效能有待进一步提高的问题。可以以这些术语为支点、以线上平台或线下实体为载体，向社会公众普及法治文化。本书以中英文对照的形式出版，希望术语所具有的时代性、简易性、趣味性能够激发域外读者的阅读兴趣，使其与中国法治文化产生共鸣，增加其对中国法治文化的理解和认同。

本书编委会

2022 年 9 月

Introduction

Key Concepts in Traditional Chinese Rule of Law Culture is a selection that offers interpretations of well-chosen key terms of traditional Chinese legal culture. It is the latest achievement guided by Xi Jinping Thought on the Rule of Law and grounded on the socialist rule of law theory with Chinese characteristics.

I. Main Content

Key Concepts in Traditional Chinese Rule of Law Culture consists of three parts, that is, legal philosophy, legal system and legal culture. The first part pulls together from various sources terms reflecting the symbolic views, ideas and theories of spiritual civilization in the formation and development of rule of law; the second part contains terms reflecting the typical mechanisms, systems and other forms of institutional civilization in the process; the third part includes terms relating to the formation and development of the rule of law culture, including signs, symbols, instruments, facilities, et cetera.

II. Principles for Selection

Key Concepts in Traditional Chinese Rule of Law Culture comprises 107 words or phrases that reflect traditional Chinese legal culture. Three major principles are followed. Firstly, the selected terms are those that have been widely used and highly recognizable in daily practice. Secondly, they have taken hold in both history and practice. Thirdly, they embody the spirit of modern jurisprudence to a certain extent.

III. Criteria for Compilation

The compilation of the terms follows five criteria. Firstly, brevity. The connotations of the terminologies should be academically rigorous and expressed in simple and intuitive language. Secondly, clarity. The description should be accurate, without ambiguity or major theoretical dispute in content. Thirdly, positive orientation. The content should be positive and in line with the requirements for promoting socialist core values. Fourthly, alignment with actual needs. The interpretation of the connotations should meet the actual needs of building a law-based country, government and society by 2035. Fifthly, easy for dissemination. The content and form should be in line with popular reading habits to ensure acceptability of the terms.

IV. Form of Presentation

The terms are presented as a compilation of entries, including the name of the term, the theoretical connotations (concept, origin, development, value, significance, et cetera) and citations, all with English translation.

The terms are generally short in form, but rich in content. Their dissemination will greatly help to improve the effectiveness of legal education. These terms can serve as key points in popularizing the rule of law culture to the public both online and offline. Furthermore, the dissemination of these traditional, simple and lively terms through translation to other parts of the world will effectively stimulate the interest of readers outside China, making it possible for them to resonate with, better understand and recognize Chinese rule of law culture.

The Editorial Board
September 2022

前　言

在旷古悠久的历史长河中，中华法治文明涌现出了灿若繁星的思想、制度和文化。这些智慧成果既是中华民族屹立于世界民族之林的稳固根基，也是中华民族不断前进的重要动力。传统法治文化集中展现了中华法治文明的精华。所谓"传统法"是今人用现代法理论对历史上已经静止了的、随时代已成为"过去"的古代法的一种诠释。[1] 与之类似，传统法治文化是今人运用现代法学理论对古代法律思想、制度和文化进行诠释的结果。中国传统法治在发展历程中积累了足以与任何其他古文明媲美的宝贵财富，其中蕴含着与现代法治理念相同的智慧精华。相关研究也应重新发掘和诠释古代法内涵，使之在当今社会重新焕发生机。

我国高度重视传统法治文化的传承和研究。2021年4月，中共中央办公厅、国务院办公厅印发《关于加强社会主义法治文化建设的意见》，再次强调了传统法文化的重要意义，指出："推动中华优秀传统法律文化创造性转化、创新性发展。传承中华法系的优秀思想和理念，研究我国古代法制传统和成败得失，挖掘民为邦本、礼法并用、以和为贵、明德慎罚、执法如山等中华传统法律文化精华，根据时代精神加以转化，加强研究阐发、公共普及、传承运用，使中华优秀传统法律文化焕发出新的生命力。"2022年2月，习近平总书记在《求是》杂志发表重要文章《坚持走中国特色社会主义法治道路 更好推进中国特色社会主义法治体系建设》，强调："要总结我国法治体系建设和法治实践的经验，阐发我国优秀传统法治文化，讲好中国法治故事，提升我国法治体系和法治理论的国际影响力和话语权。"

---

[1] 参见马小红：《礼与法：法的历史连接》，北京大学出版社2004年版，第66页。

有鉴于此，我们编写了"中国传统法治文化术语"，并将之分为"思想理念""法律制度"和"法律文化"三部分。如果将中国传统法治文化想象成一座宏伟建筑，那么"思想理念"是它的地基，"法律制度"是钢筋结构，"法律文化"是外观装饰，三者缺一不可。我们希望通过这样三个部分的讲述，使读者能够在脑海中建造一座属于中国传统法治文化的"华厦"。此外，借助于术语研究的最新成果，我们拓宽了选择术语的来源，除了专业性词汇或短语，像"王子犯法，与庶民同罪"这样流传已久且为人熟知的俗语、谚语也是重要资源。[2]

"思想理念"部分选取了 38 条术语，以勾勒出中国传统法治文化的基本面貌。从整体上来看，中国传统法律更加注重"润物细无声"的德礼教化。"明德慎罚""和为贵""德主刑辅"等人们耳熟能详的概念正体现了中国古代儒家正统法思想的精华。此外，为了尽可能展现中国传统法治文化的多样性，我们也选取了其他思想流派中标志性的法概念，如法家"法不阿贵"，道家"法令滋彰，盗贼多有"等。这些术语体现了中国传统法治文化的丰富内涵。

"法律制度"部分选取了 34 条术语，既包括"矜老恤幼""存留养亲""准五服以制罪"等体现传统社会兼顾法理和人情思维的术语，也包括"换推""鞫谳分司"等具有现代法治意义的术语，力图全面展现中国古代法律制度的实际状况。我们希望通过解读法律制度术语，使人们不但能了解中国古代制度运行的实际情况和基本特点，也能更好地认识制度背后的历史文化渊源。

"法律文化"部分共选取 35 条术语，从细微处展现中国传统法治文化的实态。法律文化渗透进中国人生活的方方面面，在器物、文本、俗语中都有体现。"情有可矜""官清法正""网开一面"等法律文化术语不但具有极高的法律专业价值，在日常生活中也被广泛使用且深入人心。这些

---

[2] 参见郑述谱：《从更宏阔的视角认识术语外译》，载《中华思想文化术语学术论文集》（第一辑）2018 年版，第 274—282 页。

术语拨开云雾进入当今研究者的视野，已成为衔接古今法治理念与文化观念的重要桥梁。

研究中国传统法治文化既是重新打磨古代法精神的系统工程，也是探寻现代中国法治思想源流的寻根之旅。我们希望通过梳理相关术语揭示中国传统法治文化的独特魅力，为重新思考中华文明的理论内涵、建设中国法治文化、建构中国法治话语、讲好中国法治故事提供理论素材。[3]

编者

2022 年 9 月

---

[3] 参见李德顺：《中华文明与中国话语》，载《中国政法大学学报》2022 年第 2 期，第 5—11 页。

Preface

Throughout its long history, the Chinese rule of law civilization has been enriched by a plethora of brilliant ideas, systems and cultures. These achievements of wisdom are not only the solid foundation for China to stand among the nations of the world, but an important driving force for the steady progress of the Chinese nation. The traditional culture of rule of law encapsulates the essence of the Chinese rule of law civilization. Generally speaking, the so-called "traditionalization" is an interpretation of the static and "old" law by people of today using modern legal theory.[1] Similarly, the traditional rule of law culture is enhanced by contemporary interpretation of ancient legal philosophy, institutions and culture using modern legal theories. In the course of its development, the traditional rule of law of China, containing the same wisdom as the modern concept, has accumulated a valuable wealth of resources comparable to that of any other ancient civilization. Relevant research should re-discover and re-interpret the connotations of ancient law for reference in today's society.

China has attached great importance to the inheritance and research of traditional legal culture. In April 2021, the General Office of the CPC Central Committee and the General Office of the State Council issued *The Opinions on Strengthening the Construction of Socialist Rule of Law Culture* (hereafter *The Opinions*), which once again stressed the significance of traditional legal culture. *The Opinions* pointed out that efforts should be made to promote the creative transformation and innovative development of China's excellent traditional legal culture, to inherit and carry forward the excellent ideas and concepts of the Chinese legal system, to study the ancient legal traditions and their successes and failures, to review in detail the essence of traditional Chinese legal culture, such as "people are the foundation of the state," "unification of rites and laws," "harmony is most precious," "the illustration of virtue and the cautious use of punishments" and "enforce the law unwaveringly," and to explore, popularize and apply in practice the essence of traditional Chinese legal culture in view of the needs of the times, so as to revitalize the excellent traditional Chinese legal culture. In February 2022, General Secretary Xi Jinping published the important article "Adhering to the Path of Socialist Rule of Law with Chinese Characteristics and Advancing the Development of the

---

[1] See Ma Xiaohong, *Li and Law: The Historic Connection of the Law*, Peking University Press, 2004, p. 66.

System of Socialist Rule of Law with Chinese Characteristics" in the journal *Qiushi*, stressing that it is necessary to summarize the experience of China in rule of law system construction and practice, elucidate China's excellent traditional rule of law culture, tell the story of China in exercising rule of law, and enhance the international influence and discourse power of China's rule of law system and theory.

Accordingly, we have compiled *Key Concepts in Traditional Chinese Rule of Law Culture*, which consists of three parts, that is, Legal Philosophy, Legal System and Legal Culture. If the traditional Chinese culture of rule of law is envisaged as a magnificent building, then the legal philosophy is the foundation; the legal system is the steel structure, and the legal culture is the exterior decoration. The three are inseparable and indispensable. We hope that with our interpretation of terms in those three parts, readers can build in their mind a "mansion" of unique traditional Chinese legal culture. In addition, with the help of the latest achievements of terminology research, we have managed to expand the source for selecting terms. Apart from legal jargons, long-standing and well-known sayings and proverbs such as "all offenders shall be punished by law equally, be they princes or commoners" have also become important resources.[2]

A total of 38 terms are selected for inclusion in the part of Legal Philosophy to outline the basic landscape of traditional Chinese rule of law culture. On the whole, traditional Chinese law paid more attention to spontaneous and silent moral education with virtue and rites. Concepts such as "the illustration of virtue and the cautious use of punishments," "harmony is most precious," and "morality given priority over penalty" reflect the orthodox legal thoughts of Confucianism in ancient China. Besides, iconic legal concepts from other schools of thought have been selected as well, to show the diversity of traditional Chinese rule of law culture as much as possible and to do justice to its rich connotations, for instance, the Legalist concept "the law does not favor the rich and the powerful" and the Daoist concept "the more laws and orders are made prominent, the more thieves and robbers there will be."

A total of 34 terms are selected for inclusion in the part of Legal System, including ones reflecting the emphasis on both the rigor of law and compassion within traditional Chinese society, such as "reduction or exemption of criminal responsibility in minors and the elderly," "permitting a criminal to support lineal elders" and "conviction and punishment based on *wufu*," as well as

---

2 See Zheng Shupu, "Understanding Foreign Translation of Terminology from a Broader Perspective", *Collection of Academic Papers on Chinese Ideological and Cultural Terminology*, No. 1, 2018, pp. 274-282.

ones with modern legal significance, such as "withdrawal and reelection" and "separation of *ju* and *yan*", in a bid to faithfully present the actualities of the ancient Chinese legal system. We hope that our interpretation of the terms on the legal system will acquaint readers with the actual situation and basic characteristics of the system operation in ancient China, and enable a better understanding of the underlying historical and cultural factors.

A total of 35 terms are selected for inclusion in the part of Legal Culture to offer a close-up view on the reality of traditional Chinese rule of law culture. Legal culture has penetrated all aspects of Chinese life and has found expression in artifacts, texts, and proverbs. Legal and cultural terms such as "forgivable in view of the circumstances," "clean and honest officials for fair law enforcement" and "give wrongdoers a leeway" are not only of extremely high legal value, but are also extensively used in daily life and are popular among the people. Concepts like these have come under the scrutiny of contemporary scholars and have become an important bridge linking ancient and modern philosophies of the rule of law and cultural views.

The study of traditional Chinese legal culture is not only a systematic project to re-polish ancient legal culture, but also a root-seeking journey to explore the origin of modern Chinese legal thought. We hope to reveal the unique charm of traditional Chinese rule of law culture by reviewing the terms, and to provide theoretical material for re-examining the theoretical connotations of the Chinese civilization, establishing the culture and constructing the discourse for rule of law in China, and telling stories about it.[3]

The Editors
September 2022

---

3 See Li Deshun, "On Chinese Civilization and Chinese Discourse", *Journal of CUPL*, No. 2, 2022, pp. 5-11.

目 录
Contents

第一篇　思想理念　　　　　　　　　001
Part I　Legal Philosophy

ānrén-níngguó
安人宁国 ·· 003
Providing Peace and Comfort to the People and Keeping the State at Peace

《Chūnqiū》juéyù
春秋决狱 ·· 005
Adjudicating Cases According to Doctrines in *The Spring and Autumn Annals*

déběn-xíngyòng
德本刑用 ·· 007
Morality as the Foundation and Penalty as the Means

dézhǔ-xíngfǔ
德主刑辅 ·· 008
Morality Given Priority over Penalty

fá dāng qí zuì

罚当其罪 010

Punishment Commensurate with the Crime

fǎ bì míng, lìng bì xíng

法必明，令必行 011

The Laws Shall Be Just and Impartial and the Promulgated Acts Shall Be Enforced.

fǎ bù'ē guì

法不阿贵 012

The Law Does Not Favor the Rich and the Powerful.

fǎ guì jiǎn dàng

法贵简当 013

Enacting Concise and Reasonable Laws

fǎ lìng zī zhāng, dàozéi duō yǒu

法令滋彰，盗贼多有 015

The More Laws and Orders Are Made Prominent, the More Thieves and Robbers There Will Be.

fǎ shēn wú shànzhì

法深无善治 017

Too Stringent and Too Many Laws Prevent Good Governance.

fǎ yǔ shí zhuǎn zé zhì
法与时转则治·····018
Laws in Line with the Times Produce Good Governance.

fèng fǎ zhě qiáng zé guó qiáng
奉法者强则国强·····019
Strong Conformers to the Law Make the Country Strong.

héwéiguì
和为贵·····020
Harmony Is Most Precious.

jīngguó-xùmín, zhèngqízhìdù
经国序民，正其制度·····022
Creating an Orderly Society When Governing a Country Requires Improved Systems.

lǐ bù xià shùrén, xíng bù shàng dàfū
礼不下庶人，刑不上大夫·····023
Rites Do Not Extend Down to the Common People and Criminal Punishment Does Not Extend Up to the Senior Nobles.

lǐfǎ-héyī
礼法合一·····024
Unification of Rites and Laws

lǐyuè bù xīng, zé xíngfá bù zhòng
礼乐不兴，则刑罚不中 ·· 026
If Rituals and Music Do Not Flourish, Punishments Will Not Be Meted out Properly.

mínwéibāngběn
民惟邦本 ·· 028
People Are the Foundation of the State.

míngdé-shènfá
明德慎罚 ·· 029
The Illustration of Virtue and the Cautious Use of Punishments

míngxíng-bìjiào
明刑弼教 ·· 031
Making Penalties Explicit to Assist Moral Education

qīnqīn-xiāngyǐn
亲亲相隐 ·· 032
Relatives Mutually Conceal Their Misconduct.

rényìzhīfǎ
仁义之法 ·· 033
The Standards of Benevolence and Righteousness

rèn dé bù rèn xíng
任德不任刑 ·· 034
Morality-ruling over Penalty-ruling

sānyòu-sānshè

三宥三赦 ·· 036

Leniency for Three Kinds of Criminal Circumstances and Pardon for Three Kinds of Criminals

shènxíng

慎刑 ·· 038

Prudential Punishment

tiānlǐ, guófǎ, rénqíng

天理、国法、人情 ·· 040

Heavenly Principle, State Law, and Human Nature

tiānwǎng-huīhuī, shū'érbùlòu

天网恢恢，疏而不漏 ·· 041

Justice Has Long Arms.

tiānxiàzhīfǎ

天下之法 ·· 042

Universal Law

tú fǎ bù zúyǐ zìxíng

徒法不足以自行 ·· 044

Laws Alone Cannot Carry Themselves into Practice.

wángzǐ fànfǎ, yǔ shùmín tóngzuì

王子犯法，与庶民同罪 ·· 045

All Offenders Shall Be Punished by Law Equally, Be They Princes or Commoners.

wéizhèng-yǐdé

为政以德 ·· 046

Governance Based on Virtue

wúsòng

无讼 ·· 047

(A Society) Free from Litigation

xīsòng

息讼 ·· 048

Quell Litigation

xíngwúděngjí

刑无等级 ·· 050

Punishments Should Know No Degree or Grade.

yīduànyúfǎ

一断于法 ·· 052

Judging All by Law

yǒu zhìfǎ érhòu yǒu zhìrén

有治法而后有治人 ··· 053

Talents of Governance Appear After Good Laws Are Made.

zhìguó wú qí fǎ zé luàn, shǒufǎ ér bùbiàn zé shuāi

治国无其法则乱，守法而不变则衰 ····································· 055

Ruling a Country Without Laws Brings Chaos While Rigidly Following Laws Without Reform Leads to Decline.

xvi

zuìyíwéiqīng

罪疑惟轻 ··· 057

Dealing with Doubtful Crimes Lightly

第二篇　法律制度　　　　　　　　　　　　　059
Part II　Legal System

biéjí-yìcái

别籍异财 ··· 061

Separate Wealth and Separate Household

chāiguān-biétuī

差官别推 ··· 062

Transfer to Higher Authority for Retrial

cúnliú-yǎngqīn

存留养亲 ··· 064

Permitting a Criminal to Support Lineal Elders

dàlǐsì

大理寺 ··· 066

Dalisi (The Court of Judicial Review)

fānyì-biékān

翻异别勘 ··· 068

Fanyi Biekan (Retrial Regarding Overturned Confession)

gé

格 ··· 070

Ge (Ruling)

huàwàirén xiāngfàn

化外人相犯 ··· 072

Crime Among Foreign Persons

huàntuī

换推 ··· 074

Withdrawal and Reelection

jīnlǎo-xùyòu

矜老恤幼 ··· 075

Reduction or Exemption of Criminal Responsibility in Minors and the Elderly

jiǔqīng huìshěn

九卿会审 ··· 076

Joint Hearing by the Nine Ministers

jūyàn-fēnsī

鞫谳分司 ··· 078

Separation of *Ju* and *Yan*

jǔ qīng yǐ míng zhòng, jǔ zhòng yǐ míng qīng

举轻以明重，举重以明轻 ··· 080

Illustrating the Heavy with the Light, and the Light with the Heavy lìng

令 082

Ling (Ordinance)

liùlǐ

六礼 083

Six-procedure Marriage Rite

lùqiú

录囚 085

Investigating Prisoners

lǜ

律 086

Lü (Statute)

mòzhězhīfǎ

墨者之法 087

Mohist Law

qiū-dōng xíngxíng

秋冬行刑 089

Execution of Sentences in Autumn and Winter

qiūshěn

秋审 091

Autumn Trial

sāncìzhīfǎ

三刺之法 ··· 093

Three Interrogations

sānsī-tuīshì

三司推事 ··· 094

Joint Trial by Three Departments

shí'è-bùshè

十恶不赦 ··· 096

Ten Unpardonable Abominations

shì

式 ··· 098

Shi (Models)

tiānrén-héyī

天人合一 ··· 100

Heaven and Man Are United as One.

wǔfùzòu

五覆奏 ·· 102

Five Rounds of Reassessment of Death Sentences

xíng

刑 ··· 103

Xing

xíngbù

刑部 104

The Ministry of Justice

xíngmíng-mùyǒu

刑名幕友 106

Xingming Muyou (Legal Advisors)

xùxíng

恤刑 107

Penalty with Prudence

yísī-biékān

移司别勘 108

Internal Transfer for Retrial

yùshǐtái

御史台 110

The Censorate

yuēfǎ-sānzhāng

约法三章 112

Three Regulations

Zhōugōng zhìlǐ

周公制礼 113

The Duke of Zhou's Establishment of Rites

zhǔn wǔfú yǐ zhìzuì
准五服以制罪···115
Conviction and Punishment Based on *Wufu*

第三篇　法律文化　　　　　　　　　　　117
Part III　Legal Culture

dēngwéngǔ
登闻鼓···119
Dengwen Drum

《Fǎjīng》
《法经》··121
Canon of Laws

fěibàngmù
诽谤木···123
Feibangmu (Commentary Column)

fúpái
符牌··124
Tally

gàozhuàng/sùzhuàng
告状/诉状···126
Gaozhuang/Suzhuang (Pleadings)

gōngàn xiǎoshuō
公案小说 ·· 127
Public-case Novel

guānlián
官联 ··· 129
Official Couplet

guānqīng fǎzhèng
官清法正 ··· 130
Clean and Honest Officials for Fair Law Enforcement

guīju
规矩 ··· 132
Guiju (Rules and Norms)

hǔfú
虎符 ··· 133
Tiger Tally

jièshífāng
戒石坊 ··· 135
Jieshifang (Admonition Archway)

jìnshànjīng
进善旌 ··· 137
Banner for Advice

xxiii

jīngtángmù

惊堂木·····138

The Chinese Gavel

lìngqiān

令签·····139

Lingqian

míngjìng-gāoxuán

明镜高悬·····141

Bright Mirror Hung High

qìyuē

契约·····142

Contract

qíngyǒukějīn

情有可矜·····144

Forgivable in View of the Circumstances

shāngyāngfāngshēng

商鞅方升·····146

Fangsheng of Shang Yang

《Shéyù Guījiàn》

《折狱龟鉴》·····147

Sheyu Guijian (*The Reference for Deciding Cases*)

shēnmíngtíng
申明亭 149
Shenming Pavilion (Declaring Pavilion)

shéngzhīyǐfǎ
绳之以法 151
Bring to Justice

shuìhǔdì qínmù zhújiǎn
睡虎地秦墓竹简 152
Bamboo Slips from Qin Tombs in Shuihudi

sòngshī mìběn
讼师秘本 154
Private Books on the Legal Pettifogger System

《Tángliùdiǎn》
《唐六典》 156
The Six Statutes of the Tang Dynasty

《Tánglǜ Shūyì》
《唐律疏议》 158
Commentary on the Tang Code

tóngguǐ
铜匦 160
The Bronze Suggestion Box

xxv

wǎngkāi-yīmiàn
网开一面··162
Give Wrongdoers a Leeway

xièzhì
獬豸··163
Xiezhi

xíngdǐng
刑鼎··165
Penal Pot

yámen
衙门··167
Yamen

yǒulǐchéng
羑里城··169
Youli City

yìngyí
儓匦··170
Yingyi

zhāngjiāshān hànmù zhújiǎn
张家山汉墓竹简··172
Bamboo Slips from Han Tombs in Zhangjiashan

zhífǎ-rúshān

执法如山 ·· 174

Enforce the Law Unwaveringly

zhíshì

执事 ·· 176

Zhishi

术语表 List of Concepts　　　　　　　　　　　177

参考文献 References　　　　　　　　　　　　183

中国历史年代简表 A Brief Chronology of Chinese History　　187

第一篇
思想理念
Part I
Legal Philosophy

ānrén-níngguó

安人宁国

Providing Peace and Comfort to the People and Keeping the State at Peace

使百姓安乐，国家安宁。唐初治国方略。唐初，统治集团在吸取隋代骤亡教训的基础上，以儒学为纲领，兼采道家"简静"和"无为"之长，采取了一系列与民休息的政策。这在法律思想上反映为主张礼法结合，明德慎罚，用法宽仁。"安人宁国"思想为"贞观之治"奠定了基础。

The term means to give peace and comfort to the people and keep the state at peace. It was a governing strategy in the early Tang Dynasty. At that time, under the guidelines of Confucianism, the ruler drew upon the merits of "simplicity and tranquility" and "non-action" advocated by Daoism, and adopted a series of policies to give the people time to recover in view of lessons learnt from the rapid collapse of the preceding Sui Dynasty. The corresponding legal thought advocated the unification of rites and law, illustration of virtue and caution in the use of punishments, and leniency in law enforcement. The concept laid the foundation for the Golden Era of the Zhenguan Reign.

引例 Citation:

◎ 夫安人宁国，惟在于君。君无为则人乐，君多欲则人苦。（吴兢《贞观政要·务农》）

（要使人民安乐、国家安宁，关键在于国君。国君能够无为而治，人民就能安乐；国君贪得无厌，人民就要受苦。）

The key to giving peace and comfort to the people and keeping the state at peace lies with the ruler. If the ruler rules according to natural laws without unduly interfering, the people will enjoy a peaceful life; however, if the ruler rules out of greed, the people will suffer. (Wu Jing: *Important Political Affairs of the Zhenguan Reign*)

《Chūnqiū》juéyù

《春秋》决狱

Adjudicating Cases According to Doctrines in *The Spring and Autumn Annals*

古代以《春秋》等儒家经典所载"微言大义"为依据来处理政治和司法问题，是一种重要的裁判方式。"《春秋》决狱"最早为董仲舒所撰著作名称，后被世人用来概括"引经决狱"现象。"《春秋》决狱"形成于西汉武帝时期，发展于魏晋南北朝，止于隋唐，体现了儒家思想法典化的历程。

In ancient times, "great meanings in a few words" contained in Confucian classics like *The Spring and Autumn Annals* served as the basis for dealing with political and judicial issues. It was an important way of adjudication. The term "adjudicating cases according to doctrines in *The Spring and Autumn Annals*" was originally the title of a book written by Dong Zhongshu, and was later used to describe the phenomenon of "adjudicating cases with reference to classics." It originated in the reign of Emperor Wu of the Western Han Dynasty, developed in the Wei, Jin, and Southern and Northern Dynasties, and ended in the Sui and Tang dynasties, reflecting the codification of Confucian concepts.

引例 Citation:

◎ 故《春秋》之治狱，论心定罪，志善而违于法者免，志恶而合于法者诛。(桓宽《盐铁论·刑德》)

（法官按照《春秋》审理案件，是依据犯罪动机来裁断。对于动机好的人，虽然触犯了国家刑律也可以免罪，对于怀有不良动机的人，即便没有犯法也要处罚。）

The judge hears cases in accordance with *The Spring and Autumn Annals* and exercises adjudication based on the motive of criminals. Those who have *bona fide* motive may be exempted even if they violated the state law, while those having a malicious motive shall be punished even though they didn't literally break the law. (Huan Kuan: *Discourses on Salt and Iron*) déběn-xíngyòng

德本刑用

Morality as the Foundation and Penalty as the Means

将德礼作为推行政教的原则，以刑罚作为推行政教的工具。是唐代立法的基本原则，体现了唐代君主以民为本的治国思想。"德本刑用"被认为是古代法律儒家化的代表性概念。

This concept means to take morality and rites as the principle and penalty as the tool for governance. It is the fundamental principle of legislation in the Tang Dynasty, embodying the ruler's people-oriented thought of state governance at that time. It is considered a representative Confucianized concept of ancient laws.

引例 Citation:

◎ 德礼为政教之本，刑罚为政教之用，犹昏晓阳秋相须而成者也。(《唐律疏议·名例律》)

（把德礼作为推行政教的根本、刑罚用作推行政教的手段，就如黑夜与白天、春季与秋季相待而又相成。）

Taking morality and ritual as the foundation for governance and taking penalty as the means are opposite but complementary. The two are mutually complementary and reinforcing, just like day and night, or spring and autumn. (*Commentary on The Tang Code*) dézhǔ-xíngfǔ

德主刑辅

Morality Given Priority over Penalty

国家治理应以道德教化为主，以刑罚惩治为辅。从源流上来看，孔子发展了周公"明德慎罚"思想，重教化而轻刑罚。受此影响，孟子十分重视实施"仁政"的重要性。董仲舒在继承前人思想的基础上，结合"阳德阴刑"思想，塑造了完整的儒家德刑关系论。自此，儒家对德刑关系的看法趋于定型。现代学者杨鸿烈在《中国法律思想史》一书中将之概括为"德主刑辅"。"德主刑辅"说深刻影响了现代人对中国古代儒家法律思想特征的认识，是一个具有中国特色的法学概念。

Moral indoctrination shall be the primary means of state governance and punishment the supplementary means. Confucius developed the idea of "the illustration of virtue and the cautious use of punishments" proposed by the Duke of Zhou and cherished moral education while depreciating punishment. Under the impact of the idea, Mencius attached great importance to benevolent governance. On the basis of his predecessors' ideas, Dong Zhongshu combined the idea with "yang for morality and yin for punishment" to develop a comprehensive Confucian theory on the relationship between morality and punishment. Since then, the Confucian view on the relationship became established. In modern times, the scholar Yang Honglie summarized the philosophy in his book entitled *The History of Chinese Legal Thought* as "morality given priority over penalty." The philosophy has delivered a huge impact on the modern interpretation of Confucian legal thought in ancient China, and has become a legal concept with Chinese characteristics.

引例 Citation:

◎ 刑者，德之辅。（董仲舒《春秋繁露·天辨在人》）

（刑罚是道德的辅助。）

Penalty supplements morality. (Dong Zhongshu: *Luxuriant Gems of The Spring and Autumn Annals*) fádāngqízuì

罚当其罪

Punishment Commensurate with the Crime

刑罚与罪行两者应相符。唐太宗强调刑罚的轻重要与罪行的严重程度相称，只有这样才能起到惩戒作用。"罚当其罪"的思想与现代刑法中"罪刑相适应"的理念有相通之处。

Punishments shall be compatible with their respective crimes. Emperor Taizong of the Tang Dynasty emphasized that the severity of penalties shall be commensurate with the seriousness of crimes, and that only in this way can the disciplinary role of penalties be realized. The concept is similar to the modern criminal law principle of the punishment must fit the crime.

引例 Citation:

◎ 赏当其劳，无功者自退；罚当其罪，为恶者戒惧。（吴兢《贞观政要·择官》）

（奖赏要与功绩相当，没有功绩的人就会自动退避；惩罚要与罪过相称，作恶的人就会有所戒惧。）

If the reward is commensurate with the merit, those without merit will naturally back off; if the punishment is commensurate with the crime, malefactors will be deterred. (Wu Jing: *Important Political Affairs of the Zhenguan Reign*) fǎ bì míng, lìng bì xíng

法必明，令必行

The Laws Shall Be Just and Impartial and the Promulgated Acts Shall Be Enforced.

法律一定要公正严明，颁布的法令必须有效执行。春秋战国时期，法家主张"以法而治"，偏居雍州的秦国践而行之。商鞅强调"法必明，令必行"，使秦国迅速跻身强国之列，并最终促成了秦始皇统一六国。

The laws shall be just and impartial, and promulgated acts shall be effectively enforced. During the Spring and Autumn and the Warring States periods, the Legalists advocated "rule by law," which was practiced by the State of Qin, located in the remote Yongzhou. Shang Yang emphasized that "the laws shall be just and impartial and the promulgated acts shall be enforced." His reform made Qin a powerful state and helped Emperor Qin Shi Huang unify China.

引例 Citation:

◎ 法必明，令必行，则已矣。(《商君书·画策》)

（法律一定要公正严明，颁布的法令必须有效执行，那样就好了。）

It would be ideal if the laws are impartial and the promulgated acts are effectively enforced. (*The Book of Lord Shang*)

fǎbù'ēguì
法不阿贵

The Law Does Not Favor the Rich and the Powerful.

法律对一切人平等，对权贵也绝不徇情偏袒。古代法家主张，治理国家应该不分贵贱亲疏，一切依据法律规定予以奖惩。其主旨强调公正执法，法律面前，人人平等。这一主张为历代推崇，是"依法治国"思想的重要来源之一。

The law treats everyone equally, not favoring the rich and the powerful. The Legalists in ancient China argued that punishment and reward should be meted out strictly in accordance with the law, without consideration for wealth and rank or the degree of affinity. They believed in fairness in enforcing the law and treating everyone as equal before the law. This belief has been championed throughout the ages and is an important source of the notion of the rule of law.

引例 Citation:

◎法不阿贵，绳不挠曲。法之所加，智者弗能辞，勇者弗敢争。刑过不避大臣，赏善不遗匹夫。(《韩非子·有度》)

（法律不偏袒权贵，墨线不随弯就曲。法律所制裁的，即便是智者也不能推脱、勇者也不敢争辩。惩罚罪过不回避大臣，奖励善行不遗漏百姓。）

The law does not favor the rich and the powerful, as the marking-line does not bend. What the law imposes, the wise cannot evade, nor can the brave defy. Senior officials are not spared punishment for wrongdoing, just as rewards for good conduct do not bypass ordinary people. (*Hanfeizi*)

fǎguìjiǎndàng
法贵简当
Enacting Concise and Reasonable Laws

法律贵在简洁恰当。这是明代立法的基本原则之一，由明太祖朱元璋提出。"法贵简当"强调法令既要"简"，亦即文字简洁，条理清晰，老百姓看得懂、记得住，又要"当"，亦即务实求中，不可偏轻偏重，以防止官吏在执法过程中玩弄法律条文伤害民众。

Enacting concise and reasonable laws, proposed by Zhu Yuanzhang, Emperor Taizu of the Ming Dynasty, was one of the fundamental principles of legislation in the Ming Dynasty. "Concise" means that the law should be clear and logical, so that people can understand it and keep it in mind. "Reasonable" means that the law should be practical and impartial, to prevent officials from taking advantage of the provisions to the detriment of the people during enforcement.

引例 Citation:

◎ 法贵简当，使人易晓。若条绪繁多，或一事两端，可轻可重，吏得因缘为奸，非法意也。夫网密则水无大鱼，法密则国无全民，卿等悉心参究，日具刑名条目以上，吾视酌议焉。(《明史·刑法志一》)

（法律贵在简洁恰当，使人容易明白。若是条目头绪繁多，或者同一罪有两种判法，可轻可重，司法官吏就会借机谋私作弊，这不符合法律的意旨。渔网太密，则水中无大鱼；法网太密，则国内没有臣民不受刑罚。诸位悉心比较研究，每天写出些刑名条目奏上来，我亲自斟酌裁择。）

The law shall be concise, reasonable, and easily understood. If there were too many provisions, or two possible penalties for the same crime, law enforcers may take the opportunity to seek personal benefits, against the purpose of the law. If the eyes of the net are too small, there will be no big fish left in the water. Similarly, if the net of law is too tight, everyone may get punished. All of you are expected to study carefully and write out some penal provisions, to be sent to me for consideration. (*The History of the Ming Dynasty*) fǎlìng zī zhāng, dàozéi duō yǒu

法令滋彰，盗贼多有

The More Laws and Orders Are Made Prominent, the More Thieves and Robbers There Will Be.

法令越多越明晰，贼盗也就越多。这是道家反对法家"以法治国"思想的代表性观点。道家主张无为而治，反对法家的"法治"。老子认为，治国之术在于君主清心寡欲，顺应自然，垂拱而治，法家企图用立法建立社会秩序的主张，实际上本末倒置，缘木求鱼。人为法"法令滋彰，盗贼多有"与自然之法"天网恢恢，疏而不漏"形成了鲜明对照。

The more laws and orders are made prominent, the more thieves and robbers there will be. This is a representative Daoist view in opposition to the Legalist philosophy "rule by law." Daoism advocates "rule through non-action" and opposes the "rule by law" advocated by Legalism. Laozi held that the key to governing a state lies in the ruler's purification of mind and desire, conformity to nature, and restraint from undue interference, and that the Legalist attempt to establish social order by legislation is actually putting the cart before the horse, and is thus doomed to fail. The counter-productive man-made law contrasts sharply with the loose yet all-encompassing natural law.

引例 Citation:

◎ 天下多忌讳，而民弥贫；民多利器，国家滋昏；人多伎巧，奇物滋起；法令滋彰，盗贼多有。(《老子·五十七章》)

（天下的禁忌越多，老百姓就越陷于贫穷；人民的锐利武器越多，国家就越陷于混乱。人们的技巧越多，邪风怪事就越闹得厉害；法令越是森严，盗贼就越是不断地增加。）

The more restrictions there are, the poorer the people will become; the more sharp weapons the people have, the more likely chaos will ensue; the more ingenious the people are, the more strange things will happen; the more stringent the laws and orders are, the more thieves and robbers there will be. (*Laozi*) fǎ shēn wú shànzhì

法深无善治

Too Stringent and Too Many Laws Prevent Good Governance.

　　法律越繁多严苛则国家越不能达到好的治理状态。"法深无善治"是南宋陈亮对法律繁杂程度与实现善治难易关系的概括。如果繁法重刑，则百姓不得安宁，国家不能太平。立法、执法应当宽仁，如此，国家才能繁荣安定。

Overly numerous and stringent laws prevent effective governance of a state. Chen Liang of the Southern Song Dynasty summarized the relationship between the complexity of laws and the achievement of good governance. If the laws are complicated and punishments are heavy, the people will suffer and the country will be in disturbance. Legislation and law enforcement shall be lenient, so that a country can be prosperous and stable.

引例 Citation:

◎ 操权急者无重臣，持法深者无善治。(《陈亮集·补遗》)
　　（用权过于急躁苛求的人就没有持重稳固的臣下，法律越繁多严苛则国家越不能达到好的治理状态。）

A person overly demanding in the exercise of power does not have loyal ministers; a state relying too much on stringent laws cannot achieve good governance. (*Collected Works of Chen Liang*)

fǎ yǔ shí zhuǎn zé zhì
法与时转则治

Laws in Line with the Times Produce Good Governance.

法度能随着时代发展而变化，国家才能繁荣安定。韩非子认为，历史阶段不同，治国方法也应不同，法律只有顺应时代发展才能使国家得到有效治理。

Prosperity and stability can be expected in a state when the laws keep pace with the times. Hanfeizi holds that the strategy of ruling shall be suited to the specific historical stage, and effective governance can be achieved when the laws are in line with the developmental trends of the times.

引例 Citation:

◎ 法与时转则治，治与世宜则有功。(《韩非子·心度》)

（法度能随着时代的发展而进行变革，国家就能治理好；治理的措施和社会情况相适应，才能取得成效。）

If laws are adapted to the times, there will be good government. If government fits the age, there will be great accomplishment. (*Hanfeizi*) fèng fǎ zhě qiáng zé guó qiáng

奉法者强则国强

Strong Conformers to the Law Make the Country Strong.

如果治理者都依法行事，那么国家会变得更为强大。韩非子此言意在提醒治理者应当严于律己，秉公执法。与此同理，在现代社会立法者、司法者和执法者应积极运用法治思维和法治方式解决问题。

If all governors can perform their duties in accordance with the law, the country will be stronger. This observation of Hanfeizi was meant to remind rulers to exercise strict self-discipline and to enforce the law impartially. Similarly, legislators, judicial personnel and law enforcers in modern society shall solve problems by active use of law-based ideas and methods.

引例 Citation:

◎ 国无常强，无常弱。奉法者强则国强，奉法者弱则国弱。(《韩非子·有度》)

（国家不会永远富强，也不会长久贫弱。奉行法度的君主坚决，国家就会富强；奉行法度的君主软弱，国家就会贫弱。）

No country is permanently strong. Nor is any country permanently weak. If the ruler is resolute in upholding the law, the country will be strong; if the ruler is irresolute, it will be weak. (*Hanfeizi*) héwéiguì

和为贵

Harmony Is Most Precious.

以和谐为贵。"和",和谐、恰当,是在尊重事物差异性、多样性基础上的和谐共存。本指"礼"的作用就是使不同等级的人既保持一定差别又彼此和谐共存,各得其所,各安其位,相得益彰,从而实现全社会的"和而不同",为儒家处理人际关系的重要伦理原则。后泛指人与人之间、团体与团体之间、国家与国家之间和谐、和睦、和平、融洽的关系状态。它体现了中华民族反对暴力冲突、崇尚和平与和谐的"文"的精神,也深刻影响了中国人的法律观念。

Make harmony a top priority. *He* (和) indicates congruity and appropriateness. It is a state of congenial co-existence on the basis of due respect for differences and diversity. At first, this phrase referred to the role of rites / social norms—to keep citizens of distinct social status co-existing in a harmonious way, with everybody having his or her own place and staying there contentedly for mutual benefits, resulting in a "harmonious yet diverse" society. It is an important moral concept of the Confucian school in managing inter-personal relations. The term later evolved to refer in general to harmonious, congenial, peaceful, and agreeable relationships among people, groups, and states. It epitomizes the "civil" nature of the Chinese people, who oppose violent conflicts and aspire for peace and harmony. In addition, it has also profoundly affected the legal philosophy of the Chinese people.

引例 Citation:

◎有子曰:"礼之用,和为贵。先王之道,斯为美,小大由之。有所不行,

知和而和，不以礼节之，亦不可行也。"(《论语·学而》)

（有子说："礼的应用，以和谐为贵。古代君主的治国方法，可宝贵的地方就在这里，不论大事小事都依照"和"的原则去做。也有行不通的时候，如果仍一味为了和谐而和谐，而不用礼来加以节制，也是不可行的。"）

Youzi said, "Make harmony a top priority in the application of rites. That is a key feature that characterizes governance by sovereign rulers in the ancient past. Always act upon the rule of harmony, no matter whether the issue at hand is minor or major. Sometimes, however, this rule may fail to work. If one insists on seeking harmony just for the sake of harmony instead of qualifying it with rites, then there will be no hope to succeed." (*The Analects*) jīngguó-xùmín, zhèngqízhìdù

经国序民，正其制度

Creating an Orderly Society When Governing a Country Requires Improved Systems.

治理国家，使人民安然有序，就要健全各项制度。原义为"圣明的君主在位时，治理国家，整顿百姓，严明有关制度"。之后，司马光在《资治通鉴》中引用了这句话，说明制度严明之于治理国家的重要性。在现代国家，完善的制度也应是治国安邦之本。

To successfully govern a country and ensure law and order among the people, systems must be improved. The concept originally meant "a competent emperor in power would govern the country, manage the people, and clarify the systems." It was later quoted by Sima Guang in *History as a Mirror* to illustrate the great significance of a strict and clear system to state governance. In modern times, well-developed systems are also the basis for effective governance.

引例 Citation:

◎ 是以圣王在上，经国序民，正其制度。（荀悦《汉纪·前汉孝武皇帝纪一》）

（所以圣明的君主在位时，治理国家，整顿百姓，严明有关制度。）

When a competent ruler reigns, he will govern the country, manage the people, and clarify the relevant systems. (Xun Yue: *The Chronicles of the Han Dynasty*)

lǐ bù xià shùrén, xíng bù shàng dàfū
礼不下庶人，刑不上大夫

Rites Do Not Extend Down to the Common People and Criminal Punishment Does Not Extend Up to the Senior Nobles.

礼制不涉及平民，刑罚不惩罚贵族。这是汉代典籍对西周法律制度特征的概括和演绎。事实上，西周时期，礼不仅约束贵族也约束平民，刑罚也没有将贵族排除在外。所谓"礼不下庶人，刑不上大夫"只是后人加以发挥的结果。

Rites do not involve the common people while punishment does not apply to the nobles. The concept was a generalization and interpretation, found in Han-Dynasty classics, of the characteristics of the legal system of the Western Zhou Dynasty. In fact, however, during the Western Zhou Dynasty, rites applied to both the nobles and the commoners, and punishments did not exclude the nobles. Therefore, this concept is an unwarranted interpretation by subsequent generations.

引例 Citation:

◎ 礼不下庶人，刑不上大夫。刑人不在君侧。(《礼记·曲礼上》)
（礼不为下面的庶人而制，刑不为上面的大夫而制。受过刑的人不能用在国君身边。）

Rites do not extend down to the common people; criminal punishment does not extend up to the nobles; a person who has been subjected to criminal punishment cannot be allowed to assist the monarch. (*The Book of Rites*) lǐfǎ-héyī

礼法合一

Unification of Rites and Laws

礼与法合而为一。礼与法本不矛盾，可以相辅相成，一体并用。"礼法合一"常用以形容汉代之后中国法律的整体特色。从源流上来看，三代以礼为法，礼法无法区分。春秋战国至秦代，法出于礼而独立，儒法两家对立，礼与法分隔。汉代之后，儒法合流，以礼入法，重为一体。"礼法合一"是中国传统法治文化的显著特征。

Rites and laws are integrated as one. They are not contradictory, but mutually reinforcing and can be employed together. This concept is often used to describe the overall characteristics of Chinese law after the Han Dynasty. In history, rites were used as law in the Xia, Shang and Zhou dynasties. Back then, rites and laws could not be distinguished from one another. From the Spring and Autumn and the Warring States periods to the Qin Dynasty, laws became independent of rites, and Confucianism and Legalism were opposed to one another, contributing to the separation of rites and laws. After the Han Dynasty, Confucianism and Legalism merged, and rites were integrated into laws once again. The "unification of rites and laws" is a distinct feature of the traditional Chinese rule of law culture.

引例 Citation:

◎ 治之经，礼与刑，君子以修百姓宁。(《荀子·成相》)

（礼义与刑罚是治理国家的两大基本原则，君子以此自我修养和治理国家，百姓从此得到安宁。）

Rites and punishments are two basic principles for governing a state. With them, a man of virtue cultivates himself, and governs the state, bringing peace to the people. (*Xunzi*) lǐyuè bù xīng, zé xíngfá bù zhòng

礼乐不兴，则刑罚不中

If Rituals and Music Do Not Flourish, Punishments Will Not Be Meted out Properly.

礼乐制度不能实施，刑罚就不会得当。春秋后期，孔子对民不聊生的乱世重刑充满忧虑。他告诫世人，失去礼乐教化，刑罚的适用就无法做到罚当其罪，而刑罪不相侔（móu）的结果则会使人们失去善恶的判断标准而手足无措。这是古代儒家推崇礼法并用的代表性观点。

If rituals and music do not prevail, punishments will not be meted out justly. In the late Spring and Autumn Period, Confucius was worried about the severe punishments afflicting the people in the age of disorder. So he exhorted that without the cultivation of rituals and music, punishments would not be meted out fairly and properly, and the people would be deprived of criteria for telling good from evil and be at a loss of what to do. This is a representative Confucian view advocating the concurrent application of rites and law in ancient China.

引例 Citation:

◎ 名不正，则言不顺；言不顺，则事不成；事不成，则礼乐不兴；礼乐不兴，则刑罚不中；刑罚不中，则民无所错手足。(《论语·子路》)

（名称不辨正，说话就不顺当；说话不顺当，事情就做不成；事情做不成，礼乐就得不到实施；礼乐得不到实施，刑罚就不会得当；刑罚不得当，民众就无所适从。）

If the names are not rectified, one's argument will not be proper. If one's argument is not proper, nothing can be accomplished. If nothing is accomplished, rituals and music will not flourish. If rituals and music do not flourish, punishments will not be just. If punishments are not just, the people will become lost as to how to behave. (*The Analects*) mínwéibāngběn

民惟邦本

People Are the Foundation of the State.

百姓是国家之根本。"民惟邦本"是古代民本思想的源头，后经儒家继承并发扬光大。孟子的"民贵君轻"思想便是典型。

People are the foundation of the state. This concept is the origin of Chinese people-oriented thought. It was later inherited and developed by Confucianism. Mencius' philosophy that "people are more important than the monarch" is a typical outcome.

引例 Citation:

◎ 皇祖有训，民可近，不可下。民惟邦本，本固邦宁。(《尚书·五子之歌》)

（伟大的先祖有训诫，民众可以亲近，不可以疏远。民众是国家的根本，根本坚固了，国家才安宁。）

Our ancestor, Yu the Great, exhorted that (a ruler) must maintain a close relationship with the people, and must not distance himself from them. The people are the foundation upon which a state stands, and a state can enjoy peace only when its foundation is solid. (*The Book of History*) míngdé-shènfá

明德慎罚

The Illustration of Virtue and the Cautious Use of Punishments

崇尚德教，谨慎用刑。鉴于商朝滥用刑罚而亡国的教训，周天子采取了以礼教为主、慎用刑罚的统治思想，这便是"明德慎罚"。在该思想指导下，西周刑罚较先前的夏商两代更为宽缓，如规定对七岁以下的儿童和八十岁以上老人不加刑。该思想对周初稳定社会、完善制度、安定人心起到了积极作用。"明德慎罚"的主张在春秋战国时为儒家所继承，并发展为"为政以德"的德治思想。西汉正统法律思想中的"德主刑辅"也由此演化而来。

The term refers to advocating the cultivation of virtue and the exercise of caution in the use of punishments. In view of lessons learnt from the disintegration of the state due to the abuse of punishments in the Shang Dynasty, the king of the Zhou Dynasty adopted "the illustration of virtue and the cautious use of punishments" as the ruling thought, upholding that rites should be fundamental and punishments should be used carefully. Under the guidance of such a thought, punishments in the Western Zhou Dynasty were more lenient than those in the preceding Xia and Shang dynasties. For example, it was stipulated that punishments shall not be imposed on children under the age of seven and the elderly over the age of eighty. The thought played a positive role in maintaining social stability, improving the system and reassuring the people. In the Spring and Autumn and the Warring States periods, it was inherited by Confucianism, which turned it into the concept of "governance based on virtue." "Morality given priority over penalty," an orthodox legal thought of the Western Han Dynasty, also evolved from it.

引例 Citation:

◎ 惟乃丕显考文王，克明德慎罚；不敢侮鳏寡，庸庸，祇祇，威威，显民，用肇造我区夏，越我一二邦以修我西土。（《尚书·康诰》）

（只有你那英明的父亲——文王能够崇尚德教而谨慎地使用刑罚，不敢欺侮那些无依无靠的人，任用应当任用的人，尊敬应当尊敬的人，镇压应当受到镇压的人，并让庶民了解他的这种治国之道。这样，才缔造了我们小小的周国，和我们的一两个盟友共同治理好我们的西方。）

It was only your great and distinguished father, King Wen, who was able to illustrate his virtue and exercise caution in the use of punishments. He dared not belittle the helpless, employed the employable, revered the reverend, suppressed those deserving to be suppressed, and made his way of governing the state known to the people. Thus he created our humble state of Zhou, and brought about law and order to our west together with a couple of allies. (*The Book of History*) míngxíng-bìjiào

明刑弼教

Making Penalties Explicit to Assist Moral Education

刑罚是一种辅助教化的治国之道。宋代之前"明刑弼教"思想并未受到充分重视。南宋时，以朱熹为代表的儒家学者重新发掘并诠释了"明刑弼教"的思想内涵，提高了"刑"的重要性。此举为后世统治者以"弼教"为由运用刑罚提供了正当性。明代开国皇帝朱元璋正是以"明刑弼教"为口号，推行重刑主义。

Penalties are a means to govern the state, in complementation to moral education. Prior to the Song Dynasty, the idea of making penalties explicit to assist moral education didn't draw full attention. During the Southern Song Dynasty, Confucian scholars represented by Zhu Xi rediscovered and interpreted its connotations, and highlighted the role of penalties, providing justification for subsequent rulers to impose penalties on the grounds of assisting moral education. Zhu Yuanzhang, the founding emperor of the Ming Dynasty, took the concept as a slogan to practice the doctrine of severe punishment.

引例 Citation:

◎ 明于五刑，以弼五教，期于予治。(《尚书·大禹谟》)
（明白用五种刑法来辅助五常之教，合于我的统治。）

It should be understood that using five penal codes to assist five kinds of ethics is consistent with my ruling. (*The Book of History*) qīnqīn-xiāngyǐn

亲亲相隐

Relatives Mutually Conceal Their Misconduct.

法律允许一定范围内的亲属隐匿或包庇犯罪而不负刑事责任。"亲亲相隐"至少可追溯至春秋战国时期。汉代时，被正式确立为法律原则，此后历朝历代皆依循。2012年修订后的《中华人民共和国刑事诉讼法》免除了被告人父母、配偶、子女强制出庭作证的义务。此举被学界视为"亲亲相隐"思想的当代体现。

The law permits relatives of a criminal to conceal or harbor his/her crime and to be exempt from criminal responsibility to a certain degree. The concept can be traced back to at least the Spring and Autumn and the Warring States periods. It was formally established as a legal principle in the Han Dynasty, and followed by successive dynasties since then. The *Criminal Procedural Law of the People's Republic of China* revised in 2012 exempted a defendant's parents, spouse and children from the obligation to testify against him/her in court. The exemption is regarded in academic circles as a contemporary embodiment of this concept.

引例 Citation:

◎ 父为子隐，子为父隐。直在其中矣。(《论语·子路》)
（父亲为儿子隐瞒，儿子为父亲隐瞒，其中隐含着正直的道理。）

The father conceals the misconduct of the son, and in turn the son conceals his misconduct. Righteous justification is embodied this way. (*The Analects*) rényìzhīfǎ

仁义之法

The Standards of Benevolence and Righteousness

仁与义的法则、标准，也称仁义之道。董仲舒强调，推行仁爱的方法，在于爱他人，而不是爱自己；推行道义的方法，首先应该严格要求自己，而不是苛求他人。董仲舒希望当政者严格要求自己，以宽厚的态度对待别人。董仲舒的仁义之法发展了儒家仁义思想。

The term refers to principles or standards of benevolence and righteousness, also called the way of benevolence and righteousness. Dong Zhongshu emphasized that in promoting benevolence one should love others, not oneself, and that in promoting righteousness one should first be strict with oneself rather than be demanding of others. He expressed the hope that those in power could exercise stringent self-discipline but be empathetic and accommodating to others. His standards of benevolence and righteousness carried forward the Confucian thought of benevolence and righteousness.

引例 Citation:

◎ 仁之法在爱人，不在爱我；义之法在正我，不在正人。(董仲舒《春秋繁露·仁义法》)

（仁的法则在爱别人，不在爱自我；义的法则在端正自我，不在端正别人。）

The standard of benevolence lies in loving others, not the self. That of righteousness lies in correcting the self, not others. (Dong Zhongshu: *Luxuriant Gems of The Spring and Autumn Annals*)

任德不任刑

rèn dé bù rèn xíng

Morality-ruling over Penalty-ruling

重德政而不重刑罚。这是汉代董仲舒对德刑关系的看法。针对汉初因袭秦朝"刑治"所带来的弊政，董仲舒重申了儒家的德治理念，提出"任德不任刑"的法律主张。他认为君主应当实施德政，以教化作为治国的主要手段，而不应一味使用刑罚。随着儒家思想在汉代政治中的不断强化，"任德不任刑"直接促进了古代道德与政治的融合。

Morality-ruling over penalty-ruling is the view of Dong Zhongshu, a scholar of the Han Dynasty, on the relationship between virtue and punishment. To deal with the drawbacks of "penalty-ruling" passed down from the Qin Dynasty to the earlier Han Dynasty, Dong reiterated the Confucian concept of "morality-ruling" and proposed "morality-ruling over penalty-ruling." He believed that emperors should adopt moral rule, with moralization as the primary means of governance and that they should refrain from solely relying on punishment. Since Confucianism played a pivotal role in politics in the Han Dynasty, the concept sped up the integration of morality and politics in ancient China.

引例 Citation:

◎ 天道之大者在阴阳。阳为德，阴为刑；刑主杀而德主生。是故阳常居大夏，而以生育养长为事；阴常居大冬，而积于空虚不用之处。以此见天之任德不任刑也。（《汉书·董仲舒传》）

（天的运动变化规律在于阴阳。阳即德治，阴即刑罚。刑罚主张杀生，而德治主张使人生存。因此，阳常常停留在炎热的夏天，把生育滋养长大作为职事；阴常常停留在隆冬，而积蓄在空虚不被使用的地方。由此看出，上天是重德治而不重刑罚的。）

Yin and yang are the laws that guide the movement of the whole universe. Yang represents rule by virtue while yin embodies punishment. The former advocates nourishing life while the latter means destroying life. Therefore, yang prevails in summer, in which all things grow and develop. Yin prevails in winter, in which all things come into storage. This shows that nature values morality over punishment. (*The History of the Han Dynasty*) sānyòu sānshè

三宥三赦

Leniency for Three Kinds of Criminal Circumstances and Pardon for Three Kinds of Criminals

"三宥三赦"是指《周礼·秋官·司刺》规定的定罪量刑政策。"三宥"，古代对不识、过失和遗忘三种犯罪情形予以宽宥的制度。不识，即因不知法律而犯罪；过失，即因疏忽大意而犯罪；遗忘，即忘记法律规定而犯罪。"三赦"，古代对幼弱、老耄、蠢愚三种人犯罪可予以赦免的制度。幼弱，即未满七岁者；老耄，即年满八十岁者；蠢愚，即智力不健全者。"三宥三赦"是西周时期的刑法原则，体现了统治者的慎刑思想。

The term refers to the policy of conviction and sentencing regulated in *The Rites of Zhou*. Under three criminal circumstances, criminals were penalized in a lenient way: ignorance (that is, committing a crime due to ignorance of the law), negligence (that is, committing a crime due to carelessness), and obliviscence (that is, committing a crime because of having forgotten relevant provisions). In addition, children under the age of 7, elders reaching the age of 80 and the mentally deficient could be pardoned. The concept was a principle of criminal laws in the Western Zhou Dynasty, reflecting the ruler's thought of caution with the imposition of punishments.

引例 Citation:

◎ 司刺掌三刺、三宥、三赦之法，以赞司寇听狱讼。(《周礼·秋官·司刺》)
（司刑掌管三次讯问、三种宽宥、三项赦免之法，以协助大理司寇审理诉讼。）

The subordinate judicial officials are in charge of the three inquiries, leniency for three kinds of criminal circumstances and pardon for three kinds of criminals, so as to assist the Minister of Justice in hearing cases. (*The Rites of Zhou*) shènxíng

慎刑

Prudential Punishment

古代法律思想。"慎刑"是指重德轻刑，反对严刑峻法的法律原则。这一原则起源于西周时期，在唐代达到鼎盛，此后长期占据主流法律思想地位。经儒法两派深化，"慎刑"思想全面渗入古代法律运作，发展出一系列法律制度。"德主刑辅""明德慎罚""三宥三赦""罪疑惟轻""五覆奏"等便是典型。

This is an ancient legal thought and a legal principle emphasizing morality over punishment, and opposing severe punishment and stringent laws. It originated in the Western Zhou Dynasty, and was upheld as a mainstream legal thought for a long period of time after reaching its peak in the Tang Dynasty. Thanks to the promotion by Confucianism and the Legalist School, it became fully integrated into ancient legal operations, and gave rise to a series of legal principles. Among them, "morality given priority over penalty," "the illustration of virtue and the cautious use of punishments," "leniency for three kinds of criminal circumstances and pardon for three kinds of criminals," "dealing with doubtful crimes lightly" and "five rounds of reassessment of death sentences" are typical representatives.

引例 Citation:

◎ 往者有司多举奏赦前事，累增罪过，诛陷亡辜，殆非重信慎刑，洒心自新之意也。（《汉书·平帝纪》）

（从前有司奏请多涉及赦免前事者，结果是累积增加罪过，责备陷害无罪之人，这恐怕不是注重信誉慎用刑法、洗心自新的办法。）

Previously, the petitions of related departments to pardon offenders merely aggravated crimes and led to the framing of innocent people. I am afraid that is not a proper way to advocate credibility and prudent enforcement of the criminal law for criminals to turn a new leaf. (*The History of the Han Dynasty*)

tiānlǐ, guófǎ, rénqíng
天理、国法、人情
Heavenly Principle, State Law, and Human Nature

"天理"即世间万物都应遵循的自然法则,"国法"即统治者所制定的国家法律,"人情"即普罗大众内心的道德情感。中国人心中的理想法律是天理、国法、人情三位一体。判断一个人是否应当承担法律责任,应兼顾三者。这一观念对于现代中国法治思想仍有深刻影响。

Heavenly principle is the natural law to be followed by everything in the universe. State law is the law of the land made by the ruler. Human nature is the morality and emotions of the public. In the eyes of the Chinese people, the ideal law should integrate the heavenly principle, state law and human nature. All three should be considered in judging whether a person should bear legal responsibilities. The concept still has a profound influence on the rule of law thought in modern China.

引例 Citation:

◎ 等到真天理国法人情出来,天下就太平了。(刘鹗《老残游记》第十一回)

The world will be at peace when the true heavenly principles, state law and human nature are all embodied. (Liu E: *The Travels of Lao Can*) tiānwǎng-huīhuī, shū'érbùlòu

天网恢恢，疏而不漏

Justice Has Long Arms.

自然的范围广大无边，稀疏而不会有一点漏失。天网，即自然之范围，后比喻国法。"天网恢恢，疏而不漏"引申为虽然法律规定宽缓，却不会遗漏有罪之人。现在多用来警告那些企图违反法律的人。

Nature is like an all-encompassing net; sparsely meshed as it is, nothing can slip through it. The net of heaven, or the scope of nature, is later used figuratively to refer to the law of the state. This concept indicates that no one would get away with a guilty deed though the law may be lenient. Nowadays, it is usually used to warn people against tendencies to violate the law.

引例 Citation:

◎ 天之道，不争而善胜，不言而善应，不召而自来，繟（chǎn）然而善谋。天网恢恢，疏而不失。(《老子·七十三章》)

（自然的规律，是不争攘而善于得胜，不说话而善于回应，不召唤而自动来到，宽缓而善于筹策。自然的范围广大无边，稀疏而不会有一点漏失。）

The heavenly way is good at conquering without strife, responding without words, making its appearance without call, and achieving results without obvious design. The heaven's net is endless, with big meshes, yet letting nothing slip through. (*Laozi*)

tiānxiàzhīfǎ
天下之法
Universal Law

"天下之法"是为保障百姓福祉所立之法，与君主为保护一己私欲所立"一家之法"有根本不同。由明末清初思想家黄宗羲提出。该思想上承孟子民本学说，下启近代民主思想，对中国现代法治思想的形成与发展起到了促进作用。

The "universal law" is legislated to safeguard the well-being of the people, and is fundamentally different from the "law of the ruling clan" that protects the ruler's selfish desires. Proposed by Huang Zongxi, a thinker of the late Ming Dynasty and the early Qing Dynasty, this concept carried forward Mencius' philosophy of "people first," inspired modern democratic thoughts, and promoted the formation and development of modern Chinese thought on the rule of law.

引例 Citation:

◎ 后之人主，既得天下，唯恐其祚命之不长也，子孙之不能保有也，思患于未然以为之法。然则其所谓法者，一家之法，而非天下之法也。（黄宗羲《明夷待访录·原法》）

（后世的君王得天下之后，唯恐皇位维持不长久、后代子孙不能继续统治，制定法度以防患于未然。可是他们所谓的法，只是君主一家的法，而不是天下的法。）

Subsequent monarchs made laws for fear that they would lose their throne soon and their descendants could not continue to rule. But the so-called laws were merely the laws of their family, not the universal laws. (Huang Zongxi: *Waiting for the Dawn: A Plan for the Prince*) tú fǎ bù zúyǐ zìxíng

徒法不足以自行

Laws Alone Cannot Carry Themselves into Practice.

仅有良法未必能够达致善治。孟子认为法律文本不仅要形式完备，还要能够体现良好的立法精神，只有二者结合才能够达致善治。

Good governance cannot necessarily be achieved with good laws alone. Mencius believed that laws should not only be complete in textual form, but be able to reflect sound legislative spirit. Only then can good governance be achieved.

引例 Citation:

◎ 徒善不足以为政，徒法不能以自行。（《孟子·离娄上》）

（光有好心，不足以治理政治；光有好法，也不能自己实施。）

Benevolence alone is not sufficient for the exercise of government; laws alone cannot carry themselves into practice. (*Mencius*) wángzǐ fànfǎ, yǔ shùmín tóngzuì

王子犯法，与庶民同罪

All Offenders Shall Be Punished by Law Equally, Be They Princes or Commoners.

古代法谚。即便是皇帝的子孙违反了法律，也要受到与常人同样的处罚。"王子犯法，与庶民同罪"体现了古代百姓对"法律面前人人平等"的美好期盼，与现代法精神有互通之处。

This is an ancient Chinese legal proverb, meaning that even the descendants of the emperor shall be subject to the same punishments as common people for breaking the law. It embodies the ancients' wish for "equality before the law" and is in line with the spirit of modern law to some extent.

引例 Citation:

◎ 众人都道："说那里话，王子犯法，庶民同罪，这是因奸杀命的事，既犯到官，还有活命的吗？"（夏敬渠《野叟曝言》第六十七回）

The by-standers all said, "What nonsense! All offenders shall be punished by law equally, be they princes or commoners. It's a case involving murder. Nobody can be exempt from death penalty at a court trial." (Xia Jingqu: *Humble Words of a Rustic Elder*) wéizhèng-yǐdé

为政以德

Governance Based on Virtue

以道德原则执掌国政、治理国家。孔子在西周统治者一向秉承的"明德慎罚"的基础上提出了为后世儒家所遵循的"德政"理念。"德政"与"威刑"相对。"为政以德"并非不要刑法，而是突出强调道德对政治的决定作用，将道德教化视为治国的根本原则与方法。

Governance of a state should be guided by virtue. Confucius proposed this philosophy—which was upheld by Confucians after him—on the basis of "the illustration of virtue and the cautious use of punishment," an approach advocated by the rulers in the Western Zhou Dynasty. Governance based on virtue stands in contrast to rule by use of harsh punishment as a deterrent. It does not, however, exclude penal codes, but rather highlights the decisive role of virtue in governance, and regards moral edification as the fundamental principle and the essential means for governance.

引例 Citation:

◎为政以德，譬如北辰居其所，而众星共之。(《论语·为政》)

（以道德教化来治理政事，就像北极星位于天空一定的方位，而众星都环绕着它运行。）

Governance based on virtue is like the North Star taking its position in the sky, while all the other stars revolve around it. (*The Analects*) wúsòng

无讼

(A Society) Free from Litigation

解决产生狱讼的根本性社会问题，以达到预防或平息讼争之目的。春秋时期礼崩乐坏的社会现实下，孔子的"无讼"思想实质上是劝诫君主应当以仁为本，有所作为，以尽可能减少讼争。后人往往将"无讼"演绎为"没有诉讼""消除诉讼"或"使诉讼不再发生"，以期盼社会没有纠纷。

The underlying social problems should be resolved so as to prevent or quell litigation. In the Spring and Autumn Period when rites and music were in ruins, the Confucian thought of "(a society) free from litigation" was essentially intended to exhort the monarch to take benevolence as the foundation for ruling and to reduce lawsuits as much as possible. Subsequent generations tend to interpret "(a society) free from litigation" as "having no litigation," "eliminating litigation" or "forestalling litigation," hoping that there will be no disputes in society.

引例 Citation:

◎ 子曰："听讼，吾犹人也，必也使无讼乎！"(《论语·颜渊》)

（孔子说："审理诉讼，我同别人差不多。一定要使诉讼不发生才好。"）

Confucius said, "In hearing cases, I am no better than any other man. What matters is to prevent litigation in the first place." (*The Analects*) xīsòng

息讼

Quell Litigation

平息争讼。"息讼"往往是古代官方平息诉讼的一种策略。大多数官员在应对诉讼时都会采取调解息讼的策略，吴祐、海瑞等古代著名清官廉吏都是典型。总的来说，"息讼"既是儒家"无讼"思想演化的必然结果，也是为应对诉讼资源匮乏而不得已的选择。

Quelling litigation is a strategy usually adopted by judicial authorities in ancient China. Most officials would use mediation to quell litigation, as manifested in the practice of famous honest and upright officials such as Wu You and Hai Rui. Broadly speaking, "quelling litigation" is not only the inevitable result of the evolution of the Confucian concept "(a society) free from litigation," but also a last resort due to limited litigation resources.

引例 Citation:

◎ 词讼之应审者，什无四五。其里邻口角，骨肉参商细故，不过一时竞气，冒昧启讼，否则有不肖之人从中播弄。果能审理，平情明切，譬晓其人，类能悔悟，皆可随时消释。间有准理后，亲邻调处，吁请息销者，两造既归辑睦，官府当予矜全，可息便息。（汪辉祖《佐治药言·息讼》）

（对于百姓诉讼，确实应当审理的不足十分之四五。大部分都是邻里间在一些细小琐事上发生口角，一时冲动进行诉讼，或者是有居心叵测的人在中间搬弄是非挑拨诉讼。如果能够得到公正审理，阐明情理事实，使当事人双方明白事理，有所悔悟，则矛盾可以得到化解。有时批准诉状后,由亲戚邻里进行调解,申请撤回诉讼,既然当事人双方已经和解,官府也应当成全,能够平息争讼的便应当平息。)

Actually, less than four or five tenths of the people's lawsuits deserve to be heard. Most of them are filed on impulse from quarrels between neighbors over trifles, or are provoked by people with malicious intent and ulterior motives. The conflicts can be resolved if a fair trial can be ensured and the fact can be clarified so that both parties can understand and repent. Sometimes, a case may be withdrawn after being accepted because relatives and neighbors of both parties have mediated the dispute. Since both parties have agreed to an amicable settlement, the government should grant their wish to drop the case. In short, litigation should be quelled wherever applicable. (Wang Huizu: *Expostulation on Assisting the Minister to Rule*) xíngwúděngjí

刑无等级

Punishments Should Know No Degree or Grade.

法律面前没有高低贵贱之分。是战国时期商鞅提出的法思想。商鞅认为法律应具有最高权威，无论何人违反君令国法，都应毫无例外予以惩处。商鞅此举在于反对贵族特权，加强君主绝对权威，以推动变法。"刑无等级"与现代法治精神有相通之处。

There is neither lowliness nor nobleness before the law. This is a legal thought put forward by Shang Yang during the Warring States Period. Shang Yang held that law should have supreme authority and that whoever violates the ruler's order and the state law shall be punished without exception. His purpose was to oppose the privileges of the nobility and strengthen the absolute authority of the king, so as to promote political reform. The thought has something in common with the modern spirit of the rule of law.

引例 Citation:

◎ 所谓壹刑者，刑无等级。自卿相、将军以至大夫、庶人，有不从王令、犯国禁、乱上制者，罪死不赦。（《商君书·赏刑》）

（所说的统一刑罚，就是刑罚不论人们的等级。自卿相、将军到大夫再到平民，如果不服从国王的命令，违犯国家的法禁，破坏国家的制度，就是死罪，绝不赦免。）

The uniformity of punishments means that punishments should know no degree or grade. From ministers of state and generals down to officials and ordinary folk, whoever defies the king's commands, violates the interdicts of the state, or rebels against the state system should be punished by death and should not be pardoned. (*The Book of Lord Shang*) yīduànyúfǎ

一断于法

Judging All by Law

不论亲疏贵贱，一律按照法律裁判。"一断于法"系古代学者概括的法家思想特点。法家认为，法应当是评价所有人行为的客观标准，所有人都应当守法，无论身份地位高低贵贱。"一断于法"原有贬低法家之意，后世则拓展了其使用范围，将之用于描述中国人追求公平正义的法律观。

Regardless of affinity or social status, all adjudication shall be made in accordance with the law. The concept encapsulates the feature of Legalist ideas summarized by ancient scholars. According to Legalists, the law, as an objective standard for evaluating the behavior of all people, shall be followed by all, regardless of social status. Although the concept was originally meant to disparage the Legalists, later generations expanded its application to describe the Chinese view of law highlighting the pursuit of fairness and justice.

引例 Citation:

◎ 法家不别亲疏，不殊贵贱，一断于法，则亲亲尊尊之恩绝矣。(《史记·太史公自序》)

（法家不区别亲疏远近，不区分贵贱尊卑，一律依据法令来决断，那么亲亲属、尊长上的恩爱关系就断绝了。）

Legalism does not take affinity or social status into consideration, but makes judgment on the basis of decrees. Therefore, the relationship between the law breaker and the law enforcer or the respect for elders and people of higher positions are made inconsequential. (*Records of the Historian*)

yǒu zhìfǎ érhòu yǒu zhìrén
有治法而后有治人

Talents of Governance Appear After Good Laws Are Made.

先制定良好的法律，然后才会出现擅长治理的人才。"治法论"是黄宗羲法思想的核心观点，颠覆了儒家思想中重"人治"而轻"法治"的传统，在中国历史上独树一帜。在近代，"治法论"被仁人志士们视为中国现代法治思想的先声。

Good laws should be made first, then there will be talents in governance. As the core view of Huang Zongxi's thought, it subverts the Confucian tradition emphasizing "rule by man" over "rule by law" and is thus unique in Chinese history. In modern times, it was regarded by men of lofty ideals as the herald of modern Chinese thought on the rule of law.

引例 Citation:

◎ 使先王之法而在，莫不有法外之意存乎其间。其人是也，则可以无不行之意；其人非也，亦不至深刻罗网，反害天下。故曰有治法而后有治人。（黄宗羲《明夷待访录·原法》）

（假如古代圣王的法度还在，那么在法度之外还保存着立法的本意。这样的话，如果是合适的人在位，就可以自由施展他的政治理念，即使当政的不得其人，也不至于严峻苛刻地执行法律，反而为害天下。所以说，先有良好的法度，然后才能出现可以治理好天下的人才。）

If the laws made by sage kings of the previous dynasties still exist, the original intent of legislation beyond will be preserved. In this way, if the right person is in power, he will be free to practice his political philosophy. Even if he is not the right person, he cannot be too strict and harsh in the enforcement of law, to the harm of the state. Therefore, good laws should be made first, and then there could appear talents in governance. (Huang Zongxi: *Waiting for the Dawn: A Plan for the Prince*) zhìguó wú qí fǎ zé luàn, shǒufǎ ér bùbiàn zé shuāi

治国无其法则乱，守法而不变则衰

Ruling a Country Without Laws Brings Chaos While Rigidly Following Laws Without Reform Leads to Decline.

　　治理国家若没有法律就会混乱，遵守法律若不知变革就会衰落。这一思想是由先秦法家代表人物慎到提出的。一方面说明了法律在国家治理中具有关键作用，另一方面也揭示了法律应与时俱进的道理。慎到认为，统治者应"以道变法"，即根据社会实际来制定、修改法律。在现代社会，制定和修改法律也应注重维护其体系的封闭性与开放性，以求兼顾法理与人情。

A state governed without laws will be chaotic but rigid conformity to law without reform will lead to decline. Proposed by the Pre-Qin Legalist Shen Dao, the concept illustrates the key role of law in governing the state and the need for the law to keep pace with the times. According to Shen, rulers shall make and amend laws based on social realities. Similarly, in modern society, efforts should be made to maintain the rigidity and flexibility of the legal system in the formulation and revision of laws, so as to balance law and compassion.

引例 Citation:

◎ 故治国无其法则乱，守法而不变则衰。有法而行私，谓之不法。以力役法者，百姓也；以死守法者，有司也；以道变法者，君长也。（欧阳询等《艺文类聚》卷五十四）

　　（所以，治理国家若没有法律就会混乱，遵守法律若不知变革就会衰落。有法可依却徇私情、满足私欲的话，就是违反法律。以身守法是百姓的事；以死亡来捍卫法律的尊严，这是政府机关的事；根据形势的变化不断变革法制，这是国君的事情。）

Therefore, ruling a country without laws brings chaos while rigidly following laws without reform leads to decline. Bending the law for personal desires constitutes violation of the law. It is the duty of the people to observe the law; it is the responsibility of governments to defend the dignity of the law; it is the obligation of the monarch to adapt the law to actualities. (Ouyang Xun et al.: *An Anthology of Pre-Tang Dynasty Literature*) zuìyíwéiqīng

罪疑惟轻

Dealing with Doubtful Crimes Lightly

当犯罪事实不能确定时，对嫌疑人从轻处罚。"罪疑惟轻"是古人在总结已有经验基础上提炼出的经典概念。统治者宣扬该观念不仅在于标榜宽仁之政，也在于通过从轻处罚教化百姓。该思想体现了古代仁政与慎刑思想，对现代中国司法实践亦有影响。

If there is uncertainty surrounding criminal facts, the suspect shall be punished lightly. This classical concept was refined by ancient Chinese people on the basis of experience. It was promoted by rulers not only to demonstrate benevolent government, but also to educate the people through lighter punishments. Manifesting the ancient idea of benevolent government and prudential punishment, it also influenced modern Chinese judicial practices.

引例 Citation：

◎ 罪疑惟轻，功疑惟重。（《尚书·大禹谟》）
（罪行处罚轻重无法确定时，就从轻处理；功绩奖赏轻重无法确定时，就从重赏赐。）

Lighter punishment should be imposed for doubtful crimes, and higher rewards should be given in case of doubtful merit. (*The Book of History*)

第二篇
法律制度
Part II
Legal System

bréjí-yìcái

别籍异财

Separate Wealth and Separate Household

针对子孙在父母、祖父母在世时自立门户和自有财产而设置的罪名。禁止别籍异财于隋唐时开始入律。《唐律·名例律》"十恶"中"不孝"罪第一条就是"父母在，别籍异财"。此后历代法典也都明令禁止别籍异财，其目的在于维护大家族制。

This was a crime against people seeking separation from their extended families and ownership of properties with their parents or grandparents still alive. The prohibition was gradually introduced into the law in the Sui and Tang dynasties. The first crime of "failure to honor filial piety" among "the Ten Evils" in *The Tang Code* was seeking separate household and properties while one's parents were still alive. Since then, laws of subsequent dynasties had explicitly forbidden such deeds, in order to maintain the system of extended families.

引例 Citation:

◎ 诸祖父母、父母在而子孙别籍异财者，徒三年。(《唐律疏议·户婚》)

（凡祖父母、父母在世，而子孙另立户籍、分割家财的，处徒刑三年。）

Anyone seeking independent registries or separate wealth with their grandparents or parents still alive shall be sentenced to three years of imprisonment. (*Commentary on The Tang Code*) chāiguān-biétuī

差官别推

Transfer to Higher Authority for Retrial

简称"移推",古代诉讼制度。差官别推是指犯人在录问时或行刑前推翻口供或不服称冤,原审机关必须将案件报送到上级机关,由上级机关委派官员对案件重新进行审理。源于五代时期,至宋代发展成熟。该制度是"翻异别勘"的一种类型,有助于防止冤假错案的发生,为金、元、明、清诸代的申诉复审制度所吸收与继承,产生了重要影响。

This concept refers to an ancient litigation practice. Under it, the original trial agency must report a case to a higher-level agency for retrial by officials otherwise designated, when a prisoner overturns the confession or claims injustice during case review or before execution. It originated in the Five Dynasties and became mature in the Song Dynasty. As a type of "Retrial Regarding Overturned Confession," it helped prevent wrongful convictions. Later, it was inherited by the appeal review system of the Jin, Yuan, Ming and Qing dynasties, and exerted profound impacts.

引例 Citation:

◎ "制勘公事,只令于临近州府抽差司狱,其间或是亲姻,必有幸门。乞令制勘官取便抽差。"诏今后凡差官推勘公事,所要司狱取便抽差。(徐松《宋会要辑稿·刑法三》)

("考察裁决案件审理时,若遇到犯人在录问时或行刑前推翻口供或不服称冤的情形,需要委派官员重新审理,如果只能从临近机关抽派官员,则可能存在姻亲或利益关系而相互包庇,希望能够不再规定重新审理的司法机关。"诏令今后在派遣官员时可以就其方便选择司法机关。)

"In case review, if the criminal overturned his/her confession or claimed injustice during interview or before execution, a retrial shall be arranged. However, if the officials for retrial were to be seconded from agencies in the vicinity only, cover-ups because of cronyism or interest exchange might be prone to occur. Therefore, it is hoped that no judicial authority shall be specified for retrial in the future." Upon this, the emperor issued a decree, allowing the presiding official to choose the retrial authority as he/she sees fit. (Xu Song: *Compendium of Rules and Regulations of the Song Dynasty*)

cúnliú-yǎngqīn
存留养亲
Permitting a Criminal to Support Lineal Elders

古代刑事制度。该制度规定，对判处死、流、徒刑且父母或祖父母年老，又无成年子孙、期亲照料的人，准许其奉养尊亲属，直至其尊亲属终老后再执行刑罚或改判。存留养亲制度肇始于北魏，完善于唐朝，延续至明清，历时千余年之久。存留养亲制度体现了古代法律制度兼顾法理与人情的特点。

The system of permitting a criminal to support lineal elders is an ancient criminal regulation, under which a criminal sentenced to death, exile, or imprisonment was given the chance of temporarily delayed penalty execution for having dependent elderly parents or grandparents that would otherwise be left destitute, so that he could take care of them before their death. It first emerged in the Northern Wei Dynasty, was improved in the Tang Dynasty and was handed down to the Ming and Qing dynasties. This system that lasted for over one thousand years embodies the emphasis of the ancient legal system on balancing law and compassion.

引例 Citation:

◎ 诸犯死罪，若祖父母、父母年七十已上，无成人子孙，旁无期亲者，具状上请。流者鞭笞，留养其亲，终则从流，不在原赦之例。(《魏书·刑罚志》)

（死刑罪犯，如果祖父母或父母年七十岁以上，家中无成年子孙或者期亲进行赡养，可以将案情上奏皇帝；流刑罪犯，则先处以鞭笞刑，责成其回家"留养其亲"，待养老送终后，再执行刑罚。在养亲期间遇到一般赦免时，流刑不能赦免。）

As for criminals sentenced to death, if their grandparents or parents are over 70 years old and there are no other adult family member or relatives to provide care, their cases should be reported to the emperor. As for those who are to be exiled, they should be sent home to "take care of their parents or grandparents" after receiving a penalty of whipping, and the sentence will be executed after the death of their parents or grandparents. In case of a general remission during the period, pardon is not applicable for exile sentences. (*The History of Northern Wei*) dàlǐsì

大理寺

Dalisi (The Court of Judicial Review)

古代中央司法机关名称。"大理"原为司法官名，相传起源于夏。春秋战国时称"理"。北齐始设大理寺，隋唐承袭。唐代大理寺为中央最高审判机关，负责审理中央百官犯罪及京师徒刑以上案件，对刑部移送地方疑难案件有复审权。长官称为大理寺卿，位九卿之列。宋神宗元丰年间，又置大理寺狱，大理寺也恢复治理狱事的职权。元代不设大理寺，其职权划归刑部。明代将大理寺与刑部职权互易，大理寺负责复核案件，刑部则享有审判权。清承明制，1906年改大理寺为大理院，为最高审判机关，并负责解释法律、监督地方各级审判工作。

Dalisi (The Court of Judicial Review) is the name of a central judicial authority in ancient China. *Dali* was originally the title for judicial officers, said to have originated in the Xia Dynasty. During the Spring and Autumn and the Warring States periods, it was called *Li*. *Dalisi* was first established as a judicial agency in the Northern Qi Dynasty, and inherited in the Sui and Tang dynasties. As the supreme central judicial authority in the Tang Dynasty, it was in charge of criminal cases committed by officials of the central government and cases involving punishment above imprisonment in the capital city, as well as review of difficult and complicated local cases transferred by the Ministry of Justice. Its principal officer was called *Dalisi Qing* (the Minister of Judicial Review), who was among the Nine Ministers. In the Yuanfeng Reign of Emperor Shenzong in the Song Dynasty, an affiliated prison was established, and its authority to manage imprisonment was restored. In the Yuan Dynasty, *Dalisi* was once abolished, and its duties were assigned to the Ministry of Justice. During the Ming Dynasty, its duties were switched with those of the Ministry of Justice, that is, *Dalisi* was charged with reviewing cases, while the Ministry of Justice was charged with adjudication. The Qing Dynasty further improved the judicial system of the Ming Dynasty. In 1906, *Dalisi* was renamed *Daliyuan*, which served as the supreme trial authority, the interpreting agency of laws and the supervisory authority over local trials.

引例 Citation:

◎ 古谓掌刑为士，又曰理。汉景帝加"大"字，取天官贵人之牢曰大理之义。后汉后，改为廷尉，魏复为大理。南朝又名廷尉，梁改名秋卿。北齐、隋为大理，加"寺"字。龙朔改为详刑寺，光宅为司刑，神龙复改。（《旧唐书·职官志三》）

> （古代叫掌刑的为"士"，又叫"理"。汉景帝加上"大"字，取天官所说"贵人之牢叫大理"的意思。后汉以后改为"廷尉"，魏时又改为"大理"，南朝又叫"廷尉"，梁改名"秋卿"，北齐、隋代改为"大理"，加上"寺"字，唐朝龙朔时改为"详刑寺"、光宅时为"司刑"，神龙时又改回"大理寺"。）

In ancient China, the person imposing punishments was called *Shi*, or *Li*. Emperor Jing of the Han Dynasty turned the title into *Dali*, following the advice of divination officials saying that the prison for grandees should be so named. The name *Dalisi* has changed many times in history, to *Tingwei* after the Later Han Dynasty, *Dali* in the Wei Dynasty, back to *Tingwei* in the Southern Dynasties, *Qiuqing* in the Liang Dynasty, *Dalisi* in the Northern Qi and Sui dynasties, and *Xiangxingsi*, *Sixing* and back to *Dalisi* successively in the Tang Dynasty. (*The Old Tang History*) fānyì-biékān

翻异别勘

Fanyi Biekan (Retrial Regarding Overturned Confession)

古代诉讼制度。源于五代时期,至宋代发展成熟。翻异,指犯人在录问时或行刑前推翻口供或不服称冤。别勘,指由另外司法机关复审。翻异别勘,即犯人在录问口供或行刑时推翻口供提出申诉因而案件必须重新审理的制度。宋代该制度分为原审机关内的"移司别勘"和上级机关指定重审的"差官别推"两种形式。《宋刑统》规定翻异别勘以三次为限,南宋时放宽至五次。该制度有助于防止冤假错案的发生,体现了古人的司法智慧。

The term refers to an ancient litigation system originating from the Five Dynasties and reaching maturity in the Song Dynasty. *Fanyi* meant that the prisoner overturned his confession or instituted an appeal during case review or before execution. *Biekan* referred to retrial by another judicial authority. In the Song Dynasty, the system included two forms, namely, transfer to another department within the original trial authority and to another judge designated by a superior authority for retrial. According to stipulations in *The Penal Code of the Song Dynasty*, retrials regarding overturned confession were limited to three and five times in the Northern Song Dynasty and the Southern Song Dynasty respectively. Embodying ancient judicial wisdom, the system helped prevent conviction and punishment based upon unjust, false, and erroneous charges.

引例 Citation:

◎ 在法,狱囚翻异,皆委监司差官别推。若犯徒流罪,已录问后,引断翻异,申提刑司审详。如情犯分明,则行下断遣。或大情疑虑,推勘未尽,即令别勘。(徐松《宋会要辑稿·刑法三》)

（根据法律规定，犯人在录问时或行刑前推翻口供或不服称冤，都要委派监司差官重新审理。如果是处以流放的刑罚，则在记录案情并审问犯人后，引断推翻后的口供，令提刑司详细审查。如果案情清楚明了就实施刑罚，如果案情存疑尚未调查清楚，就令其他司法机关复审。）

In accordance with the law, if a prisoner overturned his confession or instituted an appeal during case review or before execution, he must be retried by a superintendent. For the penalty of imprisonment or exile, after the criminal facts were recorded and the prisoner interrogated, the overturned confession may be reviewed by the Judicial Commission in detail. If the facts were truthful and clear, the original penalty would be executed; if they were dubious and further investigation was required, another judicial authority would be ordered to organize a retrial. (Xu Song: *Compendium of Rules and Regulations of the Song Dynasty*) gé

格

Ge (Ruling)

古代法律形式。主要行于南北朝至元代。"格"的名称渊源于汉代的"科",东魏始以"格"代"科",孝静帝制定《麟趾格》。隋唐时,"格"成为四种法律形式之一。"格"的主要内涵有二:一是皇帝日常发布的修改律令或有关定罪量刑敕令的汇编,二是国家机关各部门日常工作中所必须遵循的章程。在唐代,"格"主要分为两种,颁行于天下的是"散颁格",留于官署而不普遍颁行的是"留司格"。宋代的"格"多为留司格。元代以"格"代"律","格"成为最重要的法律形式,《至元新格》成为元代首部成文法典。明清时期,"格"不再作为单独的法律形式出现。

Ge (Ruling) was an ancient legal form implemented from the Southern and Northern Dynasties to the Yuan Dynasty. With its name originating from *ke* (regulations) of the Han Dynasty, it replaced *ke* in the Eastern Wei Dynasty. For example, Emperor Xiaojing formulated *Linzhi Ge* (*Ruling of the Linzhi Hall*). In the Sui and Tang dynasties, it became one of the four legal forms. *Ge* mainly consisted of two types: one included the compilation of imperial decrees on revision of *lü* and *ling* or edicts on conviction and sentencing, and the other included the regulations followed in the daily work of various departments. In the Tang Dynasty, there were two main types of *ge*, namely, "*sanbange*" (universal ruling), which was implemented among the public and "*liusige*" (administrative ruling on office affairs), which was reserved for officials. In the Song Dynasty, "*liusige*" was dominant. In the Yuan Dynasty, *ge* replaced *lü* to become the most important legal form, and *Zhiyuan Xinge* (*New Ruling of the Zhiyuan Reign*) became its first written code. In the Ming and Qing dynasties, it was no longer used as a separate legal form.

引例 Citation:

◎ 格者，百官有司之所常行之事也。（《新唐书·刑法志》）
（格，是百官有司所常行之事。）

Ge is the routine followed by all officials and related departments. (*The New Tang History*) huàwàirén xiāngfàn

化外人相犯

Crime Among Foreign Persons

古代将居住在中国境内的外国人称作"化外人",他们之间的犯罪就是"化外人相犯"。《唐律疏议》规定,凡是外国人在唐朝境内犯罪,均应受到法律制裁。相同国籍外国人之间犯罪,则依本国法裁判。不同国籍外国人之间及外国人与中国人之间犯罪,都应依《唐律》裁判。这一规定既尊重了外国人的风俗与法律,又维护了唐朝法律适用的主权原则。有学者认为《唐律》中有关"化外人相犯"的规定属于古代国际私法的实践经验。

In ancient times, foreign persons living in China were called *Huawairen* (化外人). Their crimes against each other were called "crime among foreign persons." *Commentary on The Tang Code* stipulated that all foreigners who committed crimes in the Chinese territory should be punished in accordance with law. Crimes committed by foreigners against their fellow countrymen were judged in accordance with the law of their native country, while those committed by foreigners against foreigners of different nationalities or the Chinese were judged in accordance with *The Tang Code*. This regulation not only respected the customs and laws of foreigners but also safeguarded the sovereignty principle of China in law application. Some scholars believe that it represents ancient practical experience of international private law.

引例 Citation:

◎ 诸化外人,同类自相犯者,各依本俗法;异类相犯者,以法律论。(《唐律疏议·名例律》)

（异族的人居住在中国境内，同类自相侵犯的，依照他们本国的制度处罚；不同类相互侵犯的，按照中国的法律来判定罪刑。）

Crimes committed by foreigners living in China against their fellow countrymen shall be judged in accordance with the law of their native country; crimes committed by foreigners against foreigners of different nationalities shall be judged in accordance with Chinese laws. (*Commentary on The Tang Code*) huàntuī

换推

Withdrawal and Reelection

中国古代的法官回避制度。《唐六典》规定，若主审官员与被审者是亲戚关系，或曾为师生、官长僚佐等，或有仇怨、嫌隙，应准许其请求回避，更换他官推审。此后，历代对法官回避制度皆有规定。换推制度体现了古人的司法智慧，设置初衷与现代程序法治理念相通。

This is a recusal system for judges in ancient China. *The Six Statutes of the Tang Dynasty* stipulated that if there had been familial relationship, teacher-student relationship, governor-assistant relationship, grudges or grievances between the presiding official and the interrogee, the court should entertain the request of the presiding official for withdrawal and designate another official to take charge. Since then, there were provisions on the recusal system in all dynasties. The system embodies ancient judicial wisdom, and its original intention is in line with the modern underpinnings of procedural law.

引例 Citation:

◎ 凡鞫狱官与被鞫人有亲属、仇嫌者，皆听更之。（《唐六典·刑部郎中员外郎》）

（只要主审官员和被审理者有亲属或仇嫌关系，都允许更换。）

Replacement of the presiding official should be allowed if he is a relative of the person standing trial or if he harbors grudges against the latter. (*The Six Statutes of the Tang Dynasty*) jīnlǎo-xùyòu

矜老恤幼

Reduction or Exemption of Criminal Responsibility in Minors and the Elderly

古代主张减轻或免除未成年人、老年人刑事责任的法律原则。矜，怜悯、怜惜。西周时，法律规定七岁以下的幼小者和八十岁以上的老年人是无刑事责任能力人，不受刑事处罚。之后，历朝历代在制定和适用法律时都贯彻了宽宥老幼的精神。"矜老恤幼"原则体现了古代法律以人为本的价值关怀。

The term refers to a legal principle in ancient China advocating reducing or exempting the criminal responsibilities of minors and the elderly. Great compassion was shown through this principle. In the Western Zhou Dynasty, the law stipulated that children under the age of 7 or elders over the age of 80 should be deemed as having no capacity regarding criminal responsibility and thus should not be subject to criminal punishment. In the dynasties that followed, the spirit of leniency towards the elderly and young children was shown in the formulation and enforcement of laws. The principle manifests the people-oriented feature of laws in ancient China.

引例 Citation:

◎ 悼与耄，虽有罪，不加刑焉。(《礼记·曲礼上》)

（七岁幼儿和八九十岁的老人一样，即便有罪，也不施以刑罚。）

As for children under the age of 7, even if they are guilty of a crime, no penalty will be imposed; the principle is also applicable to elders above 80. (*The Book of Rites*)

jiǔqīng huìshěn

九卿会审

Joint Hearing by the Nine Ministers

明清时期处理重大疑难案件最高级别的法律制度。明代称"九卿圆审"。清代沿用，改称"九卿会审"，特大案件交由六部（吏、户、礼、兵、刑、工）、都察院、通政使司和大理寺九个衙门长官复查、审理和判决。判决仍需交由皇帝最后核准。参加案件审理的官员并不限于九人。九卿会审是古代恤刑思想的直接体现。

The term encompasses the highest-level legal system for handling major and difficult cases in the Ming and Qing dynasties. In the Ming Dynasty, it was called "consummate hearing by the nine ministers." In the Qing Dynasty, it was renamed to "joint hearing by the nine ministers." Serious cases were reviewed, tried, and judged by the nine ministers (namely the ministers of Personnel, Revenue, Rites, War, Justice, and Works, as well as the principal of the Censorate, the Office of Transmission, and the Court of Judicial Review). The verdict was still subject to the final approval of the emperor. The number of officials attending the trial was not restricted to nine, as might be indicated by the name. This system of joint hearing by the nine ministers directly embodied the ancient thought of caution with punishment.

引例 Citation:

◎ 外省刑名，遂总汇于按察使司，而督抚受成焉。京师笞杖及无关罪名词讼，内城由步军统领、外城由五城巡城御史完结。徒以上送部，重则奏交，如非常大狱，或命王、大臣、大学士、九卿会讯。（《清史稿·刑法志三》）

（外省刑事案件，汇总到按察使司，由督抚接受。京城内判处笞杖刑和无关罪名的案件，内城由步军统领、外城由五城巡城御史审理结案。判处徒刑以上的案件送到部里，重大案件上奏皇帝；如果有特别重大的疑难案件，就由皇帝、大臣、大学士和吏、户、礼、兵、刑、工六部，都察院，通政使司和大理寺九个衙门长官共同审讯。）

Criminal cases from local provinces were transferred to the Surveillance Commission and accepted by the Governor-General. In the capital, cases involving caning and unspecified crimes of the inner city and the outer city were handled by the Infantry Command and the Ward-inspecting Censor, respectively. Cases involving the punishment of compulsory penal servitude or above were handed over to the Ministry of Justice, and important ones were reported to the emperor. Major and difficult cases were jointly heard by the emperor, Grand Ministers, the Grand Secretariat, and the nine ministers. (*Historical Manuscript of the Qing Dynasty*) jūyàn-fēnsī

鞫谳分司

Separation of *Ju* and *Yan*

审与判分离，由专职官员分别负责。宋代，地方上的刑事审判程序分为鞫和谳两大步骤。鞫，即审理犯罪事实；谳，即定罪量刑。司法机关也相应分为鞫司和谳司。审判时，鞫谳分司，各自独立活动，不得相互干扰，以求公正。鞫谳分司标志着宋代司法文化和审判艺术达到了古代司法制度史上的高峰，遗憾的是，元、明、清三朝未能继承。

Ju (interrogation) and *yan* (adjudication) were separated and handled respectively by specialized officials. In the Song Dynasty, the local criminal trial procedure was divided into two steps, namely *ju* and *yan*. The former was the interrogation for criminal facts, and the latter was the adjudication process. The judiciary was also divided into the *Ju* Division and the *Yan* Division accordingly. During the trial, to ensure justice, the two divisions were to operate independently and not interfere with one another. The separation indicated that the judicial culture and trial art of the Song Dynasty reached the peak in the history of the ancient judicial system. Regrettably, it was not followed in the Yuan, Ming, and Qing dynasties.

引例 Citation:

◎ 狱司推鞫，法司检断，各有司存，所以防奸也。（黄淮等《历代名臣奏议》卷二百一十七）

（狱司审理犯罪事实，法司检法议刑，各机关独立活动，有效防止了因权力过度集中导致的独断专行和权力滥用。）

The interrogation division checks the criminal facts, and the judicial division decides the applicable laws and discusses punishment. The independent activities of the divisions effectively prevent arbitrariness and abuse of power due to excessive concentration of power. (Huang Huai et al.: *Memorials of Famous Officials from Past Dynasties*)

jǔ qīng yǐ míng zhòng, jǔ zhòng yǐ míng qīng
举轻以明重，举重以明轻

Illustrating the Heavy with the Light, and the Light with the Heavy

中国古代法定裁判规则。在法律无明文规定时，可比照最相似的律文，拟定罪名，加减刑罚。例如，《贼盗律》规定，入夜后无故侵入别人家中，主人立即将其杀死，不会受到任何处罚。那么，如果主人仅致其折伤，自然也应是无罪。这是举重以明轻。又规定，谋杀期亲以上尊长，应当处以死刑。那么，如果是更严重的杀伤，毫无疑问也应处以死刑。这便是举轻以明重。该规则体现了古人的司法智慧，至今也具有较高的法学方法论价值。

This statutory judgment rule of ancient China stipulated that when there are no explicit legal provisions, crimes may be determined and punishment imposed at the discretion of the judge with reference to the closest regulations. For example, *Statutes on Assault and Robbery* stipulated that the house owner who immediately killed the burglar could be exempted from punishment. So the owner would naturally not be guilty for wounding the burglar only. That is a case of "illustrating the light with the heavy." *Statutes on Assault and Robbery* also stipulated that people who murdered relatives or elders shall be sentenced to death. Then, if the circumstances were more serious, there was no doubt about a death sentence. This is "illustrating the heavy with the light." Embodying ancient judicial wisdom, this principle is still of high value for legal methodology in modern times.

引例 Citation:

◎ 诸断罪而无正条，其应出罪者，则举重以明轻……其应入罪者，则举轻以明重。(《唐律疏议·名例律》)

（凡判断无律条明文规定，其中应作出罪处置的，则要引举类近之重情属出罪之事例，以明示轻于其事者作出罪处置之正确……其中应作入罪处置的，则援引已入罪之轻例，以明示作入罪处置之正确。）

When there is no explicit legal provision, the suspect may be exempted from punishment by illustrating the light with the heavy, and may be convicted by illustrating the heavy with the light. (*Commentary on The Tang Code*) lìng

令

Ling (Ordinance)

"令"是古代最为重要的法律形式之一。"令"作为一种法律形式最早出现于西周时期。起初为律之辅助，晋代开始将"令"确立为与"律"性质迥异、地位平等的法典。隋唐时，"令"成为与"律""格""式"并行的主要法律形式。宋代之后，"令"的地位逐渐下滑，入清后完全退出中国法律史的舞台。

Ling (Ordinance), as one of the most important legal forms in ancient China, first appeared in the Western Zhou Dynasty. At first, it was intended as a complement to *lü* (statute). In the Jin Dynasty, it was turned into code, and given a status equal to *lü* but of a markedly different nature. In the Sui and Tang dynasties, *ling* became a primary form of law, on a par with *lü*, *ge*, and *shi*. After the Song Dynasty, it gradually declined in importance, and was completely obscured in the Qing Dynasty.

引例 Citation:

◎ 前主所是著为律，后主所是疏为令。《汉书·杜周传》
（从前君主认为正确的就制定成为法律，后来的君主认为正确的写下来为法令。）

The previous monarchs turned what they held to be correct into *lü*, while subsequent ones took down what they held to be correct as *ling*. (*The History of the Han Dynasty*) liùlǐ

六礼

Six-procedure Marriage Rite

古代缔结婚姻六种程序性礼仪的合称，依次为纳彩、问名、纳吉、纳征、请期、亲迎。六礼主要用于贵族士大夫，对庶民要求稍宽。在战国至汉初儒家礼制典籍《礼记·昏义》《仪礼·士昏礼》中已有规定。后经礼教经典和史书演绎，历代《户婚律》都以六礼为基本内容勘定婚姻条文。中国传统婚俗的发展轨迹，始终未脱离六礼影响。

The concept is a collective term for the six steps of marriage rite in ancient times, namely proposing, birthday matching, presenting betrothal gifts, presenting wedding gifts, picking an auspicious wedding date, and the wedding ceremony. The rituals were mainly observed by the nobility and scholar-officials, while a simplified version was followed by the common people. Stipulated in *The Book of Rites* and *Etiquette and Ceremony*, two Confucian classics on rituals from the Warring States Period to the early Han Dynasty, the concept was interpreted by ritual classics and historical records to become formally established in the marital law of all dynasties. The traditional Chinese marriage customs have evolved under the influence of the six-procedure marriage rite.

引例 Citation:

◎ 是以昏礼纳采、问名、纳吉、纳征、请期，皆主人筵几于庙，而拜迎于门外。(《礼记·昏义》)

（所以婚礼中的托媒求婚、问名占卜、通告吉兆、下聘订婚、选取吉日等程序，都由女方主人在宗庙设置座席、案几，然后亲自到庙门外拜迎男方使者。）

Therefore, during the procedures of proposing, birthday matching, presenting betrothal gifts, presenting wedding gifts, and picking an auspicious wedding date, the bride's parents would set up seats and tables in the ancestral temple, and greet the bridegroom's matchmaker at the gate. (*The Book of Rites*) lùqiú

录囚

Investigating Prisoners

亦作"虑囚",皇帝或各级官吏巡视监狱、讯察狱情,以平反错案、决遣淹滞的一项监狱管理制度。录囚萌芽于先秦时期。西汉时期,正式设置录囚制度。随后,该制度为历代效仿。明清时期,结合朝审、秋审等制度,录囚制度臻于完善。录囚制度是古代统治者推行仁政而建立的代表性制度,魏明帝、晋武帝、隋高祖、唐太宗等历代帝王都有亲自录囚的记载。

Known as *luqiu* or *lüqiu* in Chinese, "investigating prisoners" was a prison management system in which the emperor or officials at all levels inspected prisons and investigated prisoners in order to correct unjust, false, or erroneous adjudications and close long-pending cases. Germinating in the Pre-Qin Period, it was formally established in the Western Han Dynasty and followed by successive dynasties. In the Ming and Qing dynasties, it became complete, thanks to the complementary systems of palace trial and autumn trial. It was a representative system established by ancient rulers to implement benevolent governance and Emperor Ming of Wei, Emperor Wu of Jin, Emperor Wen of Sui, and Emperor Taizong of Tang were known to have investigated prisoners in person according to records.

引例 Citation:

◎ 每行县录囚徒还。(《汉书·隽不疑传》)

(每次(隽不疑)到地方州县巡视审查囚徒的罪状后返回京师。)

Every time Juan Buyi would return to the capital after investigating prisoners in local provinces and counties. (*The History of the Han Dynasty*)

lǜ
律

Lü (Statute)

古代法律形式。通过国家正式立法程序制定、颁布、实施的法律文件，具有稳定性、规范性和普遍性的特点。从源流上来看，"律"具有"法律""法令"含义，至晚不会迟于商。战国商鞅改"法"为"律"后，使之成为法典名称。除宋、元两代外，中国历代均称法典为"律"。"律"是古代最基本、最重要的法律形式。

Lü (Statute) was an ancient legal form. Legal documents formulated, promulgated, and implemented through formal legislative procedures are stable, standardized, and universally applicable. In origin, *lü* has the meaning of "law" and "decree" and dates back to no later than the Shang Dynasty. After Shang Yang in the Warring States Period changed *fa* to *lü*, *lü* began to be used in the name of codes. Except for the Song and Yuan dynasties, codes were called *lü*. *Lü* was the basic and most important legal form in ancient China.

引例 Citation:

◎ 凡律以正刑定罪，令以设范立制。(《唐六典·刑部郎中员外郎》)
　　(律用来定罪处刑，令用来设立规范制度。)

Statutes were used to convict and adjudicate, and ordinances were used to establish a normative system. (*The Six Statutes of the Tang Dynasty*) mòzhězhīfǎ

墨者之法

Mohist Law

墨家团体内的纪律，其主要原则是"杀人者死，伤人者刑"。墨家是战国初期由墨翟所创立的学派。信奉墨子学说的人称为墨者，其最高领袖称为巨子。所有墨者必须服从巨子的指挥。据记载，秦惠王时期，生活在秦国的墨家巨子腹䵍（tūn）拒绝了秦惠王特赦其子杀人的提议，依据"墨者之法"中的"杀人者死，伤人者刑"处死了自己的儿子。

Mohist Law refers to the internal discipline of the Mohist community. Its main principle is "murderers shall die, while those wounding others shall be subjected to corporeal punishment." Mohism is a school of thought founded by Mo Di in the early Warring States Period. Its followers were called Mohists and its supreme leader was called *Juzi*. All Mohists had to obey the command of *Juzi*. According to records, Fu Tun, a *Juzi* of the Qin State, refused the proposal of King Hui of Qin who suggested remission to his son for murder, and executed him in accordance with Mohist Law.

引例 Citation:

◎ 墨者之法曰："杀人者死，伤人者刑。"此所以禁杀伤人也。（《吕氏春秋·去私》）

（墨家的法则说："杀人的要偿命，伤人的要受刑。"这是为了制止人们杀伤他人。）

The Mohist Law stipulated that "the murderers shall die, while those wounding others shall be subjected to corporeal punishment." The purpose was to stop people from killing or wounding others. (*Master Lü's Spring and Autumn Annals*)

qiū-dōng xíngxíng
秋冬行刑
Execution of Sentences in Autumn and Winter

古代在秋冬季节执行死刑的制度，但只适用于一般刑事犯罪。秋冬行刑的观念早在先秦时代就已产生，《左传》《礼记》等都有记载。该说主张，春夏因万物生长而适合行赏，秋冬因肃杀萧条而适合行刑。汉代董仲舒据此提出，统治者在司法实践活动中也应坚持符合阴阳顺逆和四时运行规律的原则。董仲舒此说为汉代及其后历代统治者所肯定，秋冬行刑遂成为定制。秋冬行刑体现了中国传统文化中天人合一的自然观和法律观。

This is a regulation of ancient China stipulating that capital sentences should be executed in Autumn and Winter, but it was only applied to general criminal offenses. Emerging in the Pre-Qin Period, it was recorded in *Zuo's Commentary on The Spring and Autumn Annals* and *The Book of Rites*. It holds that Spring and Summer are suitable for rewarding because they are the seasons for growth, while Autumn and Winter are suitable for execution because they feature forlorn desolation. Hence Dong Zhongshu of the Han Dynasty proposed that rulers shall also follow the principles of yin and yang and the law of the four seasons in judicial practice. His theory was affirmed by rulers of the Han Dynasty and subsequent dynasties, and execution in Autumn and Winter became a standard practice. The principle reflected the naturalist and jural view that "heaven and man are united as one" in traditional Chinese culture.

引例 Citation:

◎ 庆为春，赏为夏，罚为秋，刑为冬。（董仲舒《春秋繁露·四时之副》）
（奖励应在春季，赏赐应在夏季，惩罚应在秋季，刑戮应在冬季。）

Award in spring; reward in summer; punish in autumn, and execute in winter. (Dong Zhongshu: *Luxuriant Gems of The Spring and Autumn Annals*)

qiūshěn
秋审
Autumn Trial

　　清代实行的死刑案件复审制度，因在每年秋季举行而得名。清律规定，除犯严重危害国家统治罪名应立即处决外，其余则应暂判斩监候或绞监候，延至秋天由刑部会同大理寺、都察院等有关官员进行复审。秋审结果有情实、缓决、可矜、留养承祀四类。奏请皇帝裁决后，除情实者处以死刑外，其余皆免死。秋审制度表明古代统治者对于实施死刑的审慎态度。

Autumn trial was a review system for death sentence cases in the Qing Dynasty, so named because it was held in autumn. The law of the Qing Dynasty stipulated that the criminals sentenced to death for seriously endangering state rule should be executed without delay, while in other cases they should be sentenced to death pending execution and imprisoned until after the autumn trial when their cases were reviewed by the Ministry of Justice, the Grand Court of Revision, and the Censorate. The results of the autumn trial included four categories, namely, capital punishment, deferred execution, worthy of compassion, and canceled execution for the sake of dependent elders. The cases were then reported to the emperor for decision, and death convicts in the first category were executed, while those of the other three categories were shown mercy. The autumn trial system showed the cautious attitude of ancient rulers towards the execution of death sentences.

　　引例 Citation:

◎ 旧制，凡刑狱重犯，自大逆、大盗决不待时外，余俱监候处决。在京有热审、朝审之例，每至霜降后方请旨处决；在外直省亦有三司秋审之例，未尝一丽死刑，辄弃于市。（《清史稿·刑法志三》）

（依照旧时制度，除去犯大逆、大盗罪立即执行死刑外，刑狱重犯都监禁等待处决。在京城有热审、朝审的惯例，每到霜降后才请皇帝降旨处决；在各地也有三司秋审的惯例，没有一判决死刑就立即执行的。）

In accordance with the old system, criminals convicted of treason and robbery were executed immediately. Other criminals were imprisoned. In the capital, there were the practices of summer trial and court trial. After Frost Descent, the emperor was petitioned to order the execution. In other places, there was also the practice of autumn trial jointly held by three departments, and no death sentence was executed immediately. (*Historical Manuscripts of the Qing Dynasty*) sāncìzhīfǎ

三刺之法

Three Interrogations

西周时期处理疑难案件的法律程序。处理疑难案件应当一问群臣、二问群吏、三问万民，之后再按照大家意见，决定对罪犯加重或减轻刑罚，以免造成冤假错案。"三刺之法"是古代慎刑思想的生动体现。

The term refers to a legal procedure for handling difficult and complex cases in the Western Zhou Dynasty. In handling such cases, the court should interrogate three groups of people, namely ministers, officials, and commoners. Their opinions were then summarized to decide on the appropriate punishment, so as to avoid miscarriage of justice. The procedure is a vivid embodiment of prudential punishment thought in ancient China.

引例 Citation:

◎ 以三刺断庶民狱讼之中：一曰讯群臣，二曰讯群吏，三曰讯万民。（《周礼·秋官·小司寇》）

（通过三次讯问来使对平民诉讼的审断正确无误：一是讯问群臣，二是讯问群吏，三是讯问民众。）

In hearing cases involving ordinary people, the court should conduct interrogations of three groups, namely ministers, officials and the public, to ensure correctness of judgment. (*The Rites of Zhou*) sānsī-tuīshì

三司推事

Joint Trial by Three Departments

唐代司法制度。遇有重大案件，由皇帝下诏敕，任命刑部、御史台、大理寺官员临时组成法庭共同审理，此即三司推事。凡被委派参与审理的一般官员，都叫"三司使"。三司推事为实现司法公正提供了制度保障，对后世影响深远，明清时期的"三法司会审"即源于此制。

This refers to a judicial system in the Tang Dynasty. For major cases, the emperor would issue an edict to appoint officials from the Ministry of Justice, the Censorate, and the Court of Judicial Review to temporarily form a court for joint trial. That was called joint trial by three departments. All general officials appointed to participate in the trial were called the "Three Judicial Commissioners." The practice guaranteed judicial fairness and had a profound impact on later generations, inspiring, for example, "the joint trial of three judicial offices" in the Ming and Qing dynasties.

引例 Citation:

◎ 有大狱，即命中丞、刑部侍郎、大理卿鞫之，谓之大三司使；又以刑部员外郎、御史、大理寺官为之，以决疑狱，谓之三司使。(王溥《唐会要》卷七十八)

（有重大案件，就令中丞、刑部侍郎、大理卿审理，称他们为大三司使。令刑部员外郎、御史、大理寺官审理，通过这样的方式来决断存疑案件，称他们为三司使。）

As for important cases, the Three Senior Judicial Officers, namely the Vice Censor-in-chief, the Deputy Minister of Justice, and the Minister of the Court of Judicial Review would be ordered to hold a joint trial. The Councilor of the Ministry of Justice, the Censor, and officials from the Court of Judicial Review were ordered to hear doubtful cases. And they were collectively known as the Three Judicial Commissioners. (Wang Pu: *Compendium of Rules and Regulations of the Tang Dynasty*) shí'è-bùshè

十恶不赦

Ten Unpardonable Abominations

古代法律规定有十种严重罪行不能赦免，包括谋反、谋大逆、谋叛、恶逆、不道、大不敬、不孝、不睦、不义、内乱。《北齐律》首定"重罪十条"。隋代《开皇律》改"重罪十条"为"十恶"，"十恶"之名自此入律，目的在于维护儒家礼教秩序。"十恶"入律对后世影响极大。现在，人们常常用"十恶不赦"来形容罪大恶极、无法饶恕。

The ancient law stipulated that there were ten serious unpardonable crimes, namely rebellion, sedition, treason, parricide, depravity, great irreverence, lack of filial piety, discord, unrighteousness, and incest. In *The Law of Northern Qi*, "the ten felonies" were stipulated. In the *Kaihuang Code* of the Sui Dynasty, they were changed to "the ten abominations" and incorporated into the law, in order to safeguard Confucian ethics. The codification had a profound impact on later generations. Nowadays, people often use "ten unpardonable abominations" to describe heinous and unforgivable crimes.

引例 Citation:

◎ 五刑之中，十恶尤切。亏损名教，毁裂冠冕，特标篇首，以为明诫。其数甚恶者，事类有十，故称"十恶"。(《唐律疏议·名例律》)

(在五刑中，对犯"十恶"罪尤其重视。这些罪行使社会上的名分和礼教亏损，损毁士大夫阶层，因此特地标在首篇，以示儆诫。构成大恶的罪行有十类，所以称作"十恶"。)

People guilty of "the ten abominations" were severely punished with the five penalties. These crimes were detrimental to social ethics and etiquette, and the scholar-official class. So they were specially marked in the first chapter as a warning. There were ten categories of such crimes, hence the name. (*Commentary on The Tang Code*) shì

式

Shi (Models)

古代法律形式。最早出现于秦。主要内容是关于国家机关办事程序、原则的规定。秦简中的《封诊式》是关于案件调查、勘验、审讯等程序及法律文书程式的规定。两汉魏晋南北朝时期，"式"与"格"没有严格的区分，西魏大统十年（544年）作《大统式》颁行天下，标志着"式"成为主要法律形式。隋唐时有四种法律形式，"式"为其中之一。该时期，"式"的内容主要是尚书省二十四司及其他部门在执行"律""令""格"的过程中各自订立的办事细则和公文程式。宋代的"式"是有关体制楷模的规定，是要求他人效法的法规。元、明、清时期，"式"的地位下降，不再是主要的法律形式。

Shi, an ancient legal form, first appeared in the Qin Dynasty. It mainly included provisions on the procedures and principles of state agencies. *The Models for Sealing and Investigating* in the Qin bamboo slips were regulations on procedures for case investigation, inquest, and interrogation, as well as the format of legal documents. From the Han through Wei and Jin to the Southern and Northern Dynasties, there was no strict differentiation between *shi* and *ge*. In the 10th year of the Western Wei Dynasty (544), *The Models of Datong* was promulgated for nationwide implementation, consolidating the status of *shi* as a main legal form. There were four legal forms in the Sui and Tang dynasties, including *shi*. During that period, the content of *shi* was mainly rules and procedures established by the 24 bureaus of the Department of Imperial Affairs and other departments in implementing *lü*, *ling*, and *ge*. *Shi* in the Song Dynasty was the model of the system to be followed by others. During the Yuan, Ming, and Qing dynasties, it declined in status and ceased to be a main legal form.

引例 Citation:

◎ 式者，其所常守之法也。(《新唐书·刑法志》)

　　(式是百官和有关部门所常守之法。)

Shi is the legal form followed by all officials and relevant departments. (*The New Tang History*) tiānrén-héyī

天人合一

Heaven and Man Are United as One.

一种认为天地人相通的世界观和思维方式。这种世界观旨在强调天地和人之间的整体性和内在联系，突出了天对于人或人事的根源性意义，表现了人在与天的联系中寻求生命、秩序与价值基础的努力。"天人合一"在历史上有不同的表现方式，如天人同类、同气或者同理等。如孟子认为通过心的反思可以知性、知天，强调心、性和天之间的统一。宋儒寻求天理、人性和人心之间的相通。老子则主张"人法地，地法天，天法道"。根据对天和人理解的不同，"天人合一"也会具有不同的意义。

The term represents a world outlook and a way of thinking which hold that heaven and earth and man being interconnected. This world outlook emphasizes the integration and inherent relationship between heaven, earth, and man. It highlights the fundamental significance of nature to man or human affairs, and describes the endeavor made by man to pursue life, order, and values through interaction with nature. The term has different ways of expression in history, such as heaven and man being of the same category, sharing the same vital energy, or sharing the same principles. Mencius, for one, believed that through mental reflection one could gain understanding of human nature and heaven, emphasizing the unity of mind, human nature, and heaven. Confucian scholars of the Song Dynasty sought to connect the principles of heaven, human nature, and the human mind. Laozi maintained that "man's law is earthly, earth's law is natural, and heaven's law is Dao." Depending on a different understanding of heaven and man, the term may have different meanings.

引例 Citation:

◎以类合之，天人一也。（董仲舒《春秋繁露·阴阳义》）

（以事类相合来看，天与人是一体的。）

In terms of integration of categories, heaven and man are one. (Dong Zhongshu: *Luxuriant Gems of The Spring and Autumn Annals*)

◎儒者则因明致诚，因诚致明，故天人合一，致学而可以成圣，得天而未始遗人。（张载《正蒙·乾称》）

（儒者则由明察人伦而通达天理之诚，由通达天理之诚而洞明世事，因此天与人相合为一，通过学习而可以成为圣人，把握天理而不曾遗失对人伦的洞察。）

A Confucian scholar is sincere because of his understanding, and he achieves understanding because of his sincerity. That is why heaven and man are united as one. One can become a sage through studies, and master heaven's law without losing understanding of man's law. (Zhang Zai: *Enlightenment Through Confucian Teachings*) wǔfùzòu

五覆奏

Five Rounds of Reassessment of Death Sentences

唐代死刑复核程序。执行死刑前须向皇帝奏报五次，请予核准。贞观五年（631年），唐太宗因错杀大理寺丞张蕴古而将核准死刑的部分程序由三覆奏改为五覆奏，并规定对违反死刑复奏程序的官员处以严厉刑罚。五覆奏制度体现了唐初慎刑思想。

This refers to the reassessment procedure regarding death sentences in the Tang Dynasty. Death sentences had to be reported to the emperor five times for approval before execution. In the fifth year of Zhenguan Reign (631), Emperor Taizong of Tang changed the procedure from three rounds of reassessment to five after the unjust execution of Zhang Yungu, the Secretary of the Judicature and Revision, and stipulated severe punishment upon officials who violated the procedure. This procedure embodied the thought of prudential punishment in the early Tang Dynasty.

引例 Citation:

◎ 自今已后，宜二日中五覆奏，下诸州三覆奏。（《旧唐书·刑法志》）
（从今以后，应在两天中五次复奏，下到各州的三次复奏。）

From now on, there shall be five rounds of reassessment of death sentences within two days, and three rounds of reassessment in the provinces. (*The Old Tang History*) xíng

刑

Xing

"刑"有两重含义：一是指刑法。夏、商、周的法皆称刑，在《禹刑》《汤刑》《九刑》等上古法律名称中，"刑"就是"法"；西周周穆王时曾作《吕刑》等，"刑"与"法"也是通用。二是指刑罚及行刑方式，墨刑、劓刑等刑罚名称中的"刑"便是此义。

Xing had two meanings. One was "law." The laws of the Xia, Shang, and Zhou dynasties were called *xing*, as in *Yuxing*, *Tangxing* and *Jiuxing*. Likewise, during the reign of King Mu of the Western Zhou Dynasty, *Lüxing* was formulated. Here, *xing* was also synonymous with "law." The other referred to penalties and means of execution, as in *moxing* (tattooing the face) and *yixing* (cutting off the nose).

引例 Citation:

◎ 夏有乱政而作《禹刑》，商有乱政而作《汤刑》，周有乱政而作《九刑》，三辟之兴，皆叔世也。(《左传·昭公六年》)

（夏朝有触犯政令的，所以制定《禹刑》；商朝有触犯政令的，所以制定《汤刑》；周朝有触犯政令的，所以制定《九刑》。这三部刑法的产生，都是在各朝衰乱的时代。）

In the Xia, Shang and Zhou dynasties, *Yuxing*, *Tangxing* and *Jiuxing* were formulated respectively to curb violation of decrees. Those three laws coincided with the chaos in the decline of their respective dynasties. (*Zuo's Commentary on The Spring and Autumn Annals*) xíngbù

刑部

The Ministry of Justice

古代中央司法机关名称，为六部之一，负责刑事案件、监狱事务。隋代开皇三年（583年），尚书省改原有都官曹为刑部。唐承隋制，刑部负责司法行政及复核大理寺及州、县必须上报的徒刑以上案件。宋因之。元代废大理寺，其职权归刑部。明代恢复大理寺，但规定刑部负责审判，大理寺负责复核。清承明制，1906年将刑部改为法部，专管全国司法行政事务，不再具有审判职能。

The Ministry of Justice was the name of the central judicial authority in ancient China. As one of the six ministries, it was responsible for handling criminal cases and penitentiary affairs. During the third year of Kaihuang (583) in the Sui Dynasty, the Department of Imperial Affairs changed the previous Section for General Administration to the Ministry of Justice. The following Tang Dynasty inherited the system and charged the Ministry of Justice with judicial administration and review of cases involving punishments above imprisonment mandatorily submitted by *Dalisi* and local counties. The Song Dynasty inherited the system of Tang. In the Yuan Dynasty, when *Dalisi* was abolished, its duties were transferred to the Ministry of Justice. When *Dalisi* was restored in the Ming Dynasty, it was charged with review of cases, as case hearing was the duty of the Ministry of Justice. The Qing Dynasty inherited the system, changing the Ministry of Justice to the Ministry of Law in 1906, and trusting it with judicial administration nationwide, but not trial.

引例 Citation:

◎ 刑部　　掌刑法、狱讼、奏谳、赦宥、叙复之事。(《宋史·职官志三》)（刑部主管刑法、诉讼、报请朝廷批示狱案件、赦免、叙用之事。）

The Ministry of Justice is in charge of the criminal law, litigation and reporting criminal cases, pardon and appointment to the imperial court for approval. (*The History of the Song Dynasty*) xíngmíng-mùyǒu

刑名幕友

Xingming Muyou (Legal Advisors)

又称刑名幕吏，官府中精通法律知识的幕僚，俗称师爷。明清时期，各级官员既面临政务繁杂的压力，也面临来自书吏、胥吏的权力挑战。有鉴于此，官员便私下雇佣既熟悉法律知识又具备行政能力的人来帮助自己断案解纷，刑名幕友应运而生。可以说，刑名幕友是明清时期地方司法活动的实际操纵者。

Xingming Muyou, which was also called *Xingming Muli*, refers to staffs well versed in law and employed by local government, commonly known as *Shiye*. During the Ming and Qing dynasties, officials at all levels faced not only pressure due to complex government affairs but also challenges from the clerks and petty officials. Therefore, they used to privately hire people with legal expertise and administrative abilities to help adjudicate cases and settle disputes. Against this backdrop, *Xingming Muyou* emerged. To some extent, they actually held the sway in local judicial activities in the Ming and Qing dynasties.

引例 Citation:

◎这人来了，就到督署去求见那位刑名师爷。(吴趼人《二十年目睹之怪现状》第七回)

Upon arrival, the man went directly to the governor's office to see the legal advisor. (Wu Jianren: *Strange Events Eye-witnessed in the Past Twenty Years*) xùxíng

恤刑

Penalty with Prudence

司法官在实施刑罚之前，应怀有怜悯之心，以使刑罚轻重适度，尽可能地减少死刑。恤刑的对象主要为鳏寡孤独和老幼妇残等社会弱势群体。历代所设赦宥、虑囚、复奏等制度都体现了恤刑思想。明清时期设立了由中央派恤刑官员前往各地审录刑囚、清理冤案的专门制度。此类官员如遇到情有可矜的犯人，可停止、减轻甚至免除其刑罚。"恤刑"体现了古代民本思想。

In imposing penalty, the magistrate shall harbor compassion, so as to ensure the aptness of the penalty, and refrain from death penalty as much as possible. The objects of such were mainly socially vulnerable groups, such as the incapacitated and the helpless, the elderly, minors, women and the disabled. The systems such as pardon, investigating prisoners and reassessment set up in successive dynasties all reflected the thought of penalty with prudence. During the Ming and Qing dynasties, a specialized system was established, whereby the central government sent officials to each place to interview prisoners so as to clear up unjust cases. Such officials could suspend, reduce, or even exempt penalties. "Penalty with prudence" embodies the people-oriented thought in ancient China.

引例 Citation:

◎ 钦哉，钦哉，惟刑之恤哉！（《尚书·舜典》）
（谨慎啊谨慎啊，刑罚要慎重啊！）

"Caution! Caution! Remember caution in imposing punishment!" (*The Book of History*) yísī-biékān

移司别勘

Internal Transfer for Retrial

古代诉讼制度。移司别勘是指遇囚犯称冤情形时，案件在原审机构内移送至另一部门重审。源于五代时期，至宋代发展成熟。北宋前期，该制度适用于录问后。宋哲宗改革后，适用于录问前。移司别勘是"翻异别勘"的一种类型，能够有效防止冤假错案。

This refers to an ancient litigation system. Internal transfer for retrial meant that when a prisoner claimed injustice, the case was transferred to another department within the original trial institution for retrial. It originated in the Five Dynasties and matured in the Song Dynasty. In the early days of the Northern Song Dynasty, it was applicable after case review, but later became applicable before case review after Emperor Zhezong's reformation. As a type of "retrial regarding overturned confession," it could effectively prevent wrongful convictions.

引例 Citation:

◎ 凡有推鞫囚狱，案成后，逐处委观察、防御、团练、军事判官，引所勘囚人面前录问，如有异同，即移司别勘。（《宋刑统》卷二十九）
（在审判案件结案后，各地都应委派观察、防御、团练、军事判官等人录问囚犯，如果囚犯推翻口供或不服称冤，就在原审机构内移送至另一部门重审。）

After concluding a trial, observers, censors, training commissioners and military supervisors shall be dispatched to interview the prisoners. If prisoners overturn their confessions or claim injustice, their case will be transferred to another department in the original trial institution for retrial. (*The Penal Code of the Song Dynasty*)

yùshǐtái
御史台
The Censorate

古代主要的监察机关。西汉已有御史府。东汉时建立御史台，是行使监察职能的专门机构。魏晋南北朝时期基本沿袭。隋唐时期，御史台为中央最高监察机关，主要职责是督察行政与司法两大系统之失，以监督百官，典正法度。明洪武十五年（1382年），改御史台为都察院。清承明制，御史台之名遂废。此外，御史台也参与司法审判。

The Censorate was the primary supervisory agency in ancient China. First established in the Western Han Dynasty as the Censor's Command, it became a specialized agency to exercise supervisory function in the Eastern Han Dynasty. The Southern and Northern Dynasties basically inherited such a system. In the Sui and Tang dynasties, the Censorate became the supreme central supervisory authority, primarily charged with handling misfeasance in the administrative and judicial systems, so as to supervise officials and standardize laws and regulations. It was renamed the Chief Surveillance Office in 1382 during the reign of Emperor Taizu of Ming. The Qing Dynasty inherited the system of the Ming Dynasty and the name of Censorate was abolished. It should be noted that the Censorate was also involved in judicial trials.

引例 Citation:

◎ 御史大夫之职，掌邦国刑宪、典章之政令，以肃正朝列；中丞为之贰。（《唐六典·御史大夫》）

（御史大夫的职责，是掌管国家的刑法宪制和各种典章的政令，以肃正朝纲；中丞为御史大夫的副职。）

The Censor-in-Chief is in charge of the criminal law, constitution and regulations to solemnize the rules and regulations of the imperial court. The Palace Aid is his deputy. (*The Six Statutes of the Tang Dynasty*) yuēfǎ-sānzhāng

约法三章

Three Regulations

刘邦进入咸阳后颁布的法令，规定仅对杀人、伤人、偷盗三种行为施以相应处罚，其他一概不究。史称"约法三章"。刘邦此举一扫秦代苛法之弊，百姓为之欢欣鼓舞。"约法三章"为刘邦建立汉王朝奠定了基础。现在，"约法三章"常指订立简明易行之法，以供立约者共同遵守。

The term refers to a decree promulgated by Liu Bang, the founding emperor of the Western Han Dynasty, after his capture of Xianyang, the capital of the Qin Dynasty. The decree stipulated that penalties should be imposed for the three crimes of killing, wounding and stealing only. It enabled Liu Bang to overcome the weaknesses of the stringent laws of the Qin Dynasty, to the delight of the common people. It also laid the foundation for establishing the Han Dynasty. This concept now often refers to the establishment of a concise and easy-to-implement covenant for the parties to follow.

引例 Citation:

◎ 与父老约，法三章耳：杀人者死，伤人及盗抵罪。(《史记·高祖本纪》)
（(高祖) 和父老约法只有三条：杀人的要处死，伤人及偷盗的要依轻重抵罪。）

Emperor Gaozu made a covenant with the people, stipulating that those guilty of murder shall be sentenced to death, and those guilty of wounding others and theft shall be punished according to the seriousness of their crimes. (*Records of the Historian*)

Zhōugōng zhìlǐ
周公制礼
The Duke of Zhou's Establishment of Rites

周初重要立法活动。在周公姬旦主持下，以周族习惯法为基础，对前代部分礼仪制度加以补充、整理而形成的一套典章制度。这些制度涉及国家治理、社会生活、行为规范等方方面面。周公法律思想对后世儒家影响极大。孔子的法思想正渊源于此。"周公制礼"是中国传统法治文化史上极为重要的事件。

The Duke of Zhou's establishment of rites was an important legislative activity in the early Zhou Dynasty. Under the guidance of Ji Dan, the Duke of Zhou, a set of rules and regulations was formed by complementing and reorganizing the previous ceremonial conventions, with the customary law of Zhou as the basis. It involved all aspects of life, such as national governance, social life, and norms of conduct. The Duke of Zhou's legal philosophy had a great influence on Confucianism and became the origin of Confucian legal thought. His establishment of rites was a very important event in the history of traditional Chinese rule of law culture.

引例 Citation:

◎ 先君周公制《周礼》曰："则以观德，德以处事，事以度功，功以食民。"（《左传·文公十八年》）

（先君周公制订《周礼》说："根据礼的法则来观察人的德行，德行的好坏表现于处置事情的是非，事情的是非用以衡量功劳的大小，依功劳大小决定取食于民的厚薄。"）

The Duke of Zhou said in formulating *The Rites of Zhou* that "one's virtue is measured by the rules of rites, and can be seen from the way one handles affairs; the way one handles affairs determines one's merits, and consequently one's rewards." (*Zuo's Commentary on The Spring and Autumn Annals*) zhǔn wǔfú yǐ zhìzuì

准五服以制罪

Conviction and Punishment Based on *Wufu*

以儒家制定的五等丧服制度为亲属之间犯罪定罪量刑的依据。五服是指死者亲属按照血缘关系之亲疏尊卑而穿戴不同等差丧服的制度。根据"准五服以制罪"原则，以尊犯卑者，关系越亲近则处罚越轻，关系越疏远则处罚越重，以卑犯尊者，反之。西晋《泰始律》首次将儒家服制引入律典，作为定罪量刑原则。该原则为后世历朝历代所继承，体现了中国传统法治文化"礼法合一"的特点。

Wufu, proposed by Confucianism, was taken as the basis for conviction and punishment for certain crimes involving family members or relatives. It refers to the system according to which relatives of the dead wear different mourning clothes based on the degree of affinity and the order of status. According to the conviction-punishment principle, if the superior infringed upon the interests of the inferior, the closer the relationship they had, the lighter the punishment would be; the more distant the relationship was, the heavier the punishment would be. As for situations in which the inferior infringed on the interests of the superior, the opposite applied. In the Jin Dynasty, *The Taishi Code* first introduced *wufu* as a principle of conviction and sentencing, in line with the feature of "unification of rites and law" in ancient China.

引例 Citation:

◎ 峻礼教之防，准五服以制罪也。(《晋书·刑法志》)

（严格礼教大防，以五服为准则裁断罪行。）

Strengthen ritual and indoctrination, and use *wufu* as the guideline to adjudicate. (*The History of the Jin Dynasty*)

第三篇
法律文化
Part III
Legal Culture

dēngwéngǔ

登闻鼓

Dengwen Drum

古代统治者悬置于朝堂外以备紧急纳谏、听冤之鼓。东汉时洛阳便设有登闻鼓，延至北魏。北魏以降，登闻鼓演变为向统治者申冤的设置，隋唐时期"挝登闻鼓"入律始成为直诉方式之一。登闻鼓制度在宋朝时更加完备。统治者设立登闻院、鼓司等专门机构处理相关事务。此后，元、明、清三代对此制度亦十分重视。登闻鼓制度开辟了一条获取民间社会信息的重要途径。"击鼓鸣冤"也成为中国人内心深处独特的文化印记。

In ancient China, a drum was placed by the ruler outside the imperial court to hear emergency advice and learn about injustice. It originated in Luoyang during the Eastern Han Dynasty, and was handed down to the Northern Wei Dynasty, when it gradually became the tool for appealing to the ruler to redress a grievance. During the Sui and Tang dynasties, "beating the *Dengwen* Drum" was incorporated into the law, and became one of the direct ways of litigation. The *Dengwen* Drum System became more complete in the Song Dynasty, when the ruler set up the *Dengwen* Academy, the Drum Division and other specialized agencies to handle related matters. The following Yuan, Ming and Qing dynasties also attached great importance to the system. The *Dengwen* Drum System served as a pioneer to obtain information about civil society. "Beating the drum to announce injustice" has also left a unique cultural mark upon the Chinese people.

引例 Citation:

◎ 即邀车驾及挝登闻鼓，若上表诉，而主司不即受者，加罪一等。(《唐律疏议·斗讼律》)

(如属拦车驾及击登闻鼓，或者上奏表申诉，而有关执掌官员不立即接受的，加重一等处罚。)

If one stops the carriage (of the emperor) or beats the *Dengwen* Drum to submit a complaint, the official in charge will be punished severely for refusing to accept it on the spot. (*Commentary on The Tang code*)

《Fǎjīng》

《法经》

Canon of Laws

《法经》是战国时魏国的李悝在总结春秋以来各诸侯国立法经验的基础上，所编撰而成的法典。它是中国历史上第一部较为系统的封建成文法典。《法经》分《盗》《贼》《囚》《捕》《杂》《具》六篇，在编撰体例上，突破了以往以颁布单行法规为主的立法形式，并确立了"以罪统刑"的原则。后世法典编撰都是在《法经》基础上发展而来，所以它对中国古代法制发展具有重大意义。

Canon of Laws is a code compiled by Li Kui from the State of Wei during the Warring States Period, based on a summary of the legislative experience of the vassal states since the Spring and Autumn Period. As the first systematic written feudal code in Chinese history, it is divided into six chapters, namely "Theft and Robbery Law," "Treason Law," "Prisoner or Extent of Justice Law," "Law of Arrest," "Miscellaneous Law" and "Law of Possession." In compilation style, it broke through the previous legislative form dominated by special regulations and established the principle of "unified punishment for crimes." As the basis for subsequent codification, the *Canon of Laws* was of great significance to the development of the legal system in ancient China.

引例 Citation:

◎ 是时承用秦汉旧律，其文起自魏文侯师李悝。悝撰次诸国法，著《法经》。(《晋书·刑法志》)

（当时沿用秦汉的旧刑律，刑律的文本是魏文侯的老师李悝起草的。李悝编集各国的刑法，著成《法经》。）

The penal laws of the Qin and Han dynasties were used at that time, and the text was drafted by Li Kui, teacher of Duke Wen of Wei in the Warring States Period. Li Kui collected the criminal laws of various states and wrote the *Canon of Laws*. (*The History of the Jin Dynasty*) fěibàngmù

诽谤木

Feibangmu (Commentary Column)

立在交通要道让过往行人刻字谏言的木柱。相传尧舜时期，统治者将一根大木柱立于居所外，让人们在上面刻写意见，此木便是诽谤木。后来，在大路口也设立了诽谤木，并在木柱上端加一横木，作为指明路站、识别道路的标志，又称"华表木"或"桓表"。此后，华表逐渐失去了谏言功能，演化为皇家建筑的专有标志。

Feibangmu was a wooden column erected on thoroughfares for people to write criticism on government policies. It is said that during the reigns of Emperor Yao and Shun, there was a big wooden column outside their respective domiciles for people to write their opinions. The wooden column was called *feibangmu*. Later, it was erected on main intersections, with a crossbar added to the top for indicating directions and routes. It came to be known as *huabiao* or *huanbiao* (the ceremonial column), gradually lost its function as an advice board and evolved into a proprietary symbol of imperial architecture.

引例 Citation:

◎ 尧置敢谏之鼓，舜立诽谤之木。(《淮南子·主术训》)

（尧帝架起鼓给要进谏的人用，舜帝树起了诽谤木让人们书写意见。）

Emperor Yao set up a drum for those who wanted to give advice on government policies, and Emperor Shun erected a commentary column for those who wanted to share their opinions. (*Huainanzi*) fúpái

符牌

Tally

朝廷发驿遣使时由官员佩戴的信物，也是各级官员表明身份的证明。古代符牌种类繁多。按作用划分，有象征职位级别的腰牌、节制兵马的兵符、守卫皇城安全的门符、用于信息传递的信牌、用于交通管理的驿符等。符牌在古代国家治理中担任着重要角色，也是严密、高效法律制度的象征。

The tally was a token worn by officials dispatched as posts or envoys by the imperial court, and a proof of identity for officials at all levels. In ancient times, there were different kinds of tallies. Depending on functions, there were waist tags symbolizing ranks, commanders' tallies for deploying troops, gate tallies for guarding the imperial city, letter tallies for transmission of information, and post tallies for traffic management. Tallies played an important role in ancient national governance and were the symbol of a strict and efficient legal system.

引例 Citation:

◎ 洪武四年五月，造用宝金符及调发走马符牌。用宝符为小金牌二，中书省、大都督府各藏其一。有诏发兵，省、府以牌入，内府出宝用之。走马符牌，铁为之，共四十，金字、银字者各半，藏之内府，有急务调发，使者佩以行。（龙文彬《明会要·舆服下》）

（洪武四年（1371年）五月，制造用宝金符、调发走马符牌。用宝符是金制的，共两枚，中书省、大都督府各有一枚。有诏令要求发兵时，中书省、大都督府凭借用宝符进入内府并将其作为信物。走马符牌是铁制的，共四十枚，其中金字符牌和银字符牌各占一半，放置在内府，有紧急事务需要调用征发人员时，使者佩戴走马符牌作为信物。）

In the fifth month of the fourth year of Hongwu (1371) in the Ming Dynasty, *yongbao* tallies and *zouma* tallies were manufactured. There were two *yongbao* tallies, one for the Central Secretariat and one for the Grand Governor's Office. When there was an imperial decree requesting the dispatch of troops, the Central Secretariat and the Grand Governor's Office would enter the imperial storehouse and use the tallies as a pledge. There were forty *zouma* tallies, all made of iron. Half of them were engraved with gold characters and half engraved with silver ones. All of them were placed in the imperial storehouse. The envoy wore it as a pledge for emergencies calling for requisition. (Long Wenbin: *Compendium of Rules and Regulations of the Ming Dynasty*)

gàozhuàng/sùzhuàng

告状/诉状

Gaozhuang/Suzhuang (Pleadings)

古代诉讼中说明事件的书状,也称"状子"。"告状",又称"告词",相当于原告起诉状。"诉状",又称"诉词",相当于被告答辩状。现在所使用的起诉状、答辩状等法律文书名称,也正是源于此。今天的"告状"早已超越法律语境而成为日常词汇。

Gaozhuang and *suzhuang* were written statements in ancient litigation, also called *zhuangzi*. *Gaozhuang*, also known as *gaoci*, was roughly the same as today's "complaint." *Suzhuang*, or *suci*, was the same as today's "answer." *Gaozhuang* and *suzhuang* were thus the respective origins of the complaint and answer used nowadays. In Chinese, *gaozhuang* has gone beyond the legal context to become a daily word.

引例 Citation:

◎ 诸鞫狱者,皆须依所告状鞫之。若于本状之外,别求他罪者,以故入人罪论。(《唐律疏议·断狱》)

(凡审问案子,都必须依所告发的罪状审问犯人。如在所告之原罪状之外,另外追问其他犯罪的,以故意判人有罪或重罪的犯罪论处。)

In every case, the criminal must be interrogated according to the crime charged with. Where s/he is interrogated beyond the original accusation, the presiding officer shall be punished for intentionally convicting a person of a crime or felony. (*Commentary on The Tang Code*) gōngàn xiǎoshuō

公案小说

Public-case Novel

宋代通俗文艺中便有"公案"之名。至明清而渐趋成熟。狭义公案小说指明代晚期集中出现的以"公案"为名的短篇小说集，如《龙图公案》《廉明公案》等，此类作品多袭自前代的法律文书、案例汇编。广义公案小说指所有包含公案内容的小说作品。清代公案小说与侠义小说合流产生了《三侠五义》《施公案》等，此类长篇作品文学性较强，在民间有较大影响。公案小说以反映冤狱为主要情节，以颂扬和赞誉"清官"为主题，清官一定意义上成为"天理"的代表。

The name *gongan* (public case) dates back to the popular literature and art of the Song Dynasty. Public-case novels gradually became mature as a literary genre in the Ming and Qing dynasties. In the narrow sense, the term "public-case novel" refers to short story collections that appeared in the late Ming Dynasty, such as *Longtu Gongan* and *Lianming Gongan*. Those works were mostly based on legal documents and case compilations of previous dynasties. In the broad sense, "public-case novel" refers to all novels about public cases. The integration of public-case novels and chivalrous novels in the Qing Dynasty gave rise to long novels such as *Three Heroes and Five Gallants* and *Shi Gongan*, which were highly influential among the people for their distinct literary features. The main plot of public-case novels features redress of wrongful cases, and the theme features praise for "clean and upright officials," who were synonymous with "heavenly justice" to some extent.

引例 Citation:

◎ 余携归阅之,笑曰:'此《龙图公案》耳,何足辱郑盦(ān)之一盼乎?'及阅至终篇,见其事迹新奇,笔意酣恣,描写既细入豪芒,点染又曲中筋节。……闲中着色,精神百倍。如此笔墨,方许作平话小说,如此平话小说,方算得天地间另是一种笔墨。(俞樾《重编〈七侠五义传〉序》)

(我将此书带回阅读,笑称"这不过是《龙图公案》罢了,怎么值得郑盦欣赏"。但阅读完全书后,我发现这本书记载故事新奇,行文酣畅淋漓,描写细致入微,点染直击要处。……不经意处的润色使得此书内容更加丰富精彩。这样的文字,才能算作平话小说;这样的平话小说,才算得上是小说创作的另一种风格。)

I brought this book home to read and smiled to myself, "This is none other than a replica of *Longtu Gongan*. Why was Zheng An full of praise for it?" However, after reading it through, I found that the story is novel; the writing is delightful; the description is meticulous, and the definitive theme is straight to the point. ...Some seemingly inadvertent touches make it even more exciting. Only such texts fit a vernacular novel; only such a vernacular novel can be regarded a distinct style in novel creation. (Yu Yue: "Preface to the Revised Edition of *Seven Heroes and Five Gallants*") guānlián

官联

Official Couplet

古代官员在官署衙门撰题的对联。最早始于宋代，明清时期逐渐兴盛。他们撰写对联并悬置官署衙门，作为施政纲领，告知民众，并以此公布自己的官风、政愿和心迹。

Official couplets were written by officials for government offices in feudal China. They first appeared in Song Dynasty and became gradually popular during the Ming and Qing dynasties. Officials wrote the couplets and hung them on the gate of their office building to inform the public of their style of government, policy agenda and aspirations.

引例 Citation:

◎ 公生明，廉生威。（[明] 郭允礼《官箴》）

（公正产生严明，清廉产生威信。）

Fairness leads to solemnity, while honesty leads to prestige. (Guo Yunli: *Official Mottos*)

guānqīng fǎzhèng
官清法正
Clean and Honest Officials for Fair Law Enforcement

官员清正廉洁，执法才能公正。这一理念在中国古代文学作品中常有表现，例如，元代李行道所撰杂剧《灰阑记》对此便有描述。剧中，马员外妻和赵令史同谋，诬告马妾张海棠害死丈夫，并抢夺海棠之子。负责审案的包拯查明真相，将孩子判归海棠。包拯正是"官清法正"的典范。"官清法正"寄托了百姓渴望公正廉明官吏的现实期盼，也折射出中国古代民间源远流长的清官情结。

Only when officials are clean and honest can law enforcement be impartial. The concept was often depicted in literary works in ancient China. For example, *The Chalk Circle*, a *zaju* play written by Li Xingdao in the Yuan Dynasty, is a case in point. In the play, Landlord Ma's wife and Magistrate Zhao conspired to falsely accuse Ma's concubine Zhang Haitang of murdering Ma and take away her son. Bao Zheng, who was in charge of the case, found out the truth and gave the boy back to Haitang. Therefore, he was regarded as a paragon of "clean and honest officials for fair law enforcement." The concept reflects the yearning of people for fair and honest officials, as well as the long-standing sentiment of ancient Chinese people for upright officials.

引例 Citation:

◎ 我这衙门里问事，真个官清法正，件件依条律的。（李行道《灰阑记》第二折）

（在我这衙门里办事的，的确是官员清廉、法律严明，每件事都是依照条律执行的。）

In my government office, all the officials are clean and honest and all laws are strictly followed, while all issues are handled according to rules. (Li Xingdao: *The Chalk Circle*) guī jǔ

规矩

Guiju (Rules and Norms)

一定的标准、法则和习惯。"规"和"矩"原本分别是矫正圆形和方形的工具，后来衍生出标准、法则、习惯等含义。孟子"不以规矩，不能成方圆"的经典论述至今被视为告诫人们做人应端正老实、做事应谨遵标准的名言警句。在当代中国，人们认为法律是治国理政最重要的规矩。

Guiju refers to certain standards, rules and customs. Originally, *gui* or "compass", and *ju* or "the carpenter's square", were tools for correcting circles and squares respectively. Later, *guiju* took on the meanings of standards, rules, and customs. Mencius' classic statement that "one would not be able to form squares and circles without a carpenter's square and compass" is still regarded as a motto to follow rules and embrace an upright life. In contemporary China, law is believed to be the most important *guiju* for national governance.

引例 Citation:

◎ 孟子曰："离娄之明，公输子之巧，不以规矩，不能成方圆。"(《孟子·离娄上》)

（孟子说："离娄虽眼神好、公输般虽有巧艺，但如果不使用圆规曲尺，也不能画出方形和圆形。"）

Mencius said, "Even with the sharp eyes of Li Lou and the superb skills of Lu Ban the master carpenter, one would not be able to form squares and circles without a carpenter's square and compass." (*Mencius*) hǔfú

虎符

Tiger Tally

古代帝王授予臣下兵权和调发军队的信物。虎形，故称"虎符"。虎符由左右两部分组成，右半边为朝廷所存，左半边由将领所持。在调动军队时由朝廷使臣检验核对，左右相合才能发兵。虎符在战国时期盛行，秦汉至隋沿用，唐朝时因避讳"虎"字而改为鱼符等形制，南宋又恢复使用虎符，此后逐渐演变为令牌。虎符在历史上是皇权的象征。

The tiger tally, known as *hufu* in Chinese, was a token used by ancient emperors to grant military authority to their officers and mobilize troops. Named after its tiger shape, it consisted of two parts. The right piece was kept by the central government, while the left piece was issued to a commander. Only upon verification of a perfect match between the two pieces by an imperial envoy could the commander mobilize troops. The tiger tally prevailed during the Warring States Period and was used from the Qin and Han dynasties to the Sui Dynasty. During the Tang Dynasty, when the Chinese character for tiger became a taboo, it was changed into the fish tally and other shapes. The tiger tally was restored in the Southern Song Dynasty and gradually evolved into a token. It was a symbol of imperial power historically.

引例 Citation:

◎ 公子诚一开口请如姬，如姬必许诺，则得虎符夺晋鄙军。(《史记·魏公子列传》)

(如若公子诚请求魏王宠妃如姬帮忙，如姬一定会答应，这样便可以窃取虎符，夺得魏将晋鄙统帅的军队。)

If you ask Lady Ru, the king's favorite consort for help, she will certainly agree to get you the tally. And once you have it, you will be able to take over Jin Bi's troops. (*Records of the Historian*) jièshífāng

戒石坊

Jieshifang (Admonition Archway)

立在衙门大堂前劝诫官吏廉洁爱民的石牌坊。北宋初年，皇帝命令各府衙在公堂前立起一块石碑，并刻上"尔俸尔禄，民膏民脂，下民易虐，上天难欺"十六个字，意在告诫官吏应廉洁奉公。后世历代沿袭，并将石碑改为了石牌坊。戒石坊体现了古代的廉政文化。

Jieshifang is a stone archway erected at the front gate of *yamen* (government offices) to admonish officials to be clean-fingered and to care about the welfare of the people. In the early years of the Northern Song Dynasty, the emperor ordered every local government office to erect a stone tablet in front of the official building with a text of 16 engraved Chinese characters, meaning "All your salaries come from commoners' hard-earned money. Commoners may be easily exploited, but the heaven is not easily deceived." The stone stele was intended as a reminder to officials to be honest in performing their duties. It was inherited in the following dynasties, and later changed to a stone archway. *Jieshifang* embodies the culture of integrity of ancient China.

引例 Citation:

◎ 左右有东西角门，再进为戒石坊、为经国堂，堂前有月台。（苏昌臣《河东盐政汇纂》卷二）

（左右两边是东西角门，再往前就是戒石坊和经国堂，经国堂前有月台。）

On the left and right sides, there are the East and West corner gates respectively, and further ahead there is the *Jieshifang* and *Jingguo* Hall. In front of the *Jingguo* Hall, there is a platform. (Su Changchen: *Compilation of Salt Administration in Hedong*) jìnshànjīng

进善旌

Banner for Advice

上古时期专为进谏良言者设立的一种标志性旗帜。尧始设进善旌，鼓励人们对政务提出建议与批评。《大戴礼记》《淮南子》等古籍对此有所记载。设置进善旌有助于统治者广泛听取臣民的意见，避免决策失误。

The term refers to a symbolic banner for encouraging advice to the emperor. Instated by Emperor Yao to encourage advice regarding government affairs, it is recorded in *Dai the Elder's Book of Rites*, *Huainanzi* and other classics. It helped rulers to solicit public opinions extensively and to avoid mistakes in decision-making.

引例 Citation:

◎ 古之治天下，朝有进善之旌，诽谤之木，所以通治道而来谏者。(《史记·孝文本纪》)

（古代治理天下，朝廷设有进良言用的旌旗和批评朝政的木牌，是为了开通治道，招徕进谏之人。）

In ancient times, the imperial court set up a banner to encourage advice and a wooden board to encourage criticism on government policies, in order to solicit advice on state governance. (*Records of the Historian*) jīngtángmù

惊堂木

The Chinese Gavel

古代官员在审理案件过程中用来拍打桌案，以震慑受审者、维持秩序的长方形小硬木块，功能与法槌相似。惊堂木早在春秋战国时期便开始使用，清代后淡出历史舞台。惊堂木是彰显衙门司法权威的法律器物，因小说、戏曲中常用这一意象而为普通民众所熟悉。

The term refers to a wooden block used by an official to call for order during case hearing, similar to the gavel in function. It began to be used in the Spring and Autumn and the Warring States periods and gradually disappeared in the Qing Dynasty. As a legal implement to highlight the judicial authority of government offices, it became familiar to the general public due to frequent appearance in novels and operas.

引例 Citation:

◎ 只见包公把惊堂木一拍，一声断喝。（石玉昆《三侠五义》第五回）

Bao Zheng banged the gavel against the desk, and bellowed a thunderous shout. (Shi Yukun: *Three Heroes and Five Gallants*) lìngqiān

令签

Lingqian

衙门审案时，主官向下属发布指令所用的签牌。清代时，衙门公案上放置两个签筒，分别放着红头（又称火签）、绿头签牌（又称签票），前者是用刑签，后者是缉拿签。令签本为木质，装在公案上的签筒中，主官需要发布指令时，就从签筒中抽出一枚扔到堂下，后经发展出现了纸质签票。主官抛掷令签以彰显法庭威严，并凸显判决结果具有强制执行力。在古代社会，令签既是司法实践中不可或缺的器物，也是体现司法权威的象征。令签在古代小说中经常出现，是民众认识审判程序的符号之一。

Lingqian were wooden or bamboo slips used by magistrates to issue orders to their subordinates in the course of trials. During the Qing Dynasty, two buckets were placed on the desk, holding red-headed slips (known as *huoqian*) and green-headed slips (known as *qianpiao*) respectively. The former were used for imposing punishment, and the latter were used for making arrests. When the magistrate needed to issue an order, he would pick up a slip and throw it onto the ground. Later, paper slips appeared. The magistrate threw slips to show the authority of the court and to suggest the enforceability of his verdict. In ancient society, *lingqian* was not only an indispensable instrument in judicial practice, but also a symbol of judicial authority. Often appearing in ancient novels, it was one of the symbols acquainting the public with the trial procedure.

引例 Citation:

◎ 祁太爷立即拈了一枝火签，差原差立拿凤鸣岐，当堂回话。（吴敬梓

《儒林外史》第五十一回）

The Prefect Qi picked up a red-headed bamboo slip, and ordered some runners to summon Feng Mingqi to the court at once for questioning. (Wu Jingzi: *The Scholars*) míngjìng-gāoxuán

明镜高悬

Bright Mirror Hung High

古代衙门公堂之上常挂匾额的内容。古人常用"明镜高悬"来形容官员断案公正严明。晋代葛洪《西京杂记》卷三记载,相传秦始皇有一面镜子,能照见人心善恶。后人以"秦镜高悬"来比喻官员明察是非。后经过民间戏曲作品演绎,"秦镜高悬"逐渐变为通俗易懂的"明镜高悬"。

Four Chinese characters literally meaning "bright mirror hung high" were inscribed on the horizontal plaque usually hung aloft in the official hall. The term was often used to describe an official as just and fair in case hearing. According to Vol. 3 of *Miscellaneous Records of the Western Capital* compiled by Ge Hong in the Jin Dynasty, Emperor Qin Shi Huang had a mirror that could see through people's mind, so later generations used "the mirror of Qin hung high" metaphorically to refer to a discerning official. After adaptation by folk operas, "the mirror of Qin hung high" gradually evolved into the more vernacular "bright mirror hung high."

引例 Citation:

◎ 只除非天见怜,奈天天又远,今日个幸对清官,明镜高悬。(关汉卿《望江亭》第四折)

(只能依靠上天垂怜,但奈何天又远不可及,现在有幸遇到一个清官,能够明察秋毫、秉公断案。)

What I can do now is to pray that the heaven would have mercy on me, but it is so far away. How lucky I am to meet an honest and upright official who is discerning, prudent and able to handle cases fairly! (Guan Hanqing: *The Riverside Pavilion*) qìyuē

契约

Contract

人们在社会交往中形成的各种文字协议。中国是世界上契约发达最早的国家之一。现存最早的契约是《五祀卫鼎铭文》等四份刻在青铜器上的铭文。经过历代发展，中国古代社会出现了种类繁多、形式各异的契约，但万变不离其宗，人们使用契约的目的都是划定彼此的权利与义务，以稳定各种社会关系。广泛使用契约的历史经验证明了中国人自古以来就具有诚实守信的美德。

Contracts refer to various written agreements formed among people during social interactions. China is one of the earliest countries with well-developed contracts worldwide. The earliest existing contracts are four texts inscribed on bronze wares, including the *Inscription of the Wei Tripod*. Throughout the ages, a wide variety of contracts in different forms appeared in ancient China, but the purpose was always to delineate rights and obligations in order to stabilize various social relationships. The extensive use of contracts in history proves that the Chinese people have upheld the virtues of honesty and credibility since ancient times.

引例 Citation:

◎ 武宁节度使王德用自陈所置马得于马商陈贵，契约具在。（司马光《涑水记闻》卷十）

（武宁节度使王德用自称从马商陈贵处购得此马，买卖契约都有。）

Wang Deyong, the Military Governor of Wuning, claimed to have bought the horse from Chen Gui, a horse trader, and to have the contract of sale. (Sima Guang: *Records of Tales by a Native of Sushui*) qíngyǒukějīn

情有可矜

Forgivable in View of the Circumstances

依情理可被宽恕。清代秋审对于虽身犯死刑但因情理可被减刑的人的判决结果。也被称为"可矜""可疑""事有可疑"等。"情有可矜"案件通常是指老幼废疾等人犯罪、因救护父母而伤他人性命等情形的案件。凡被判为"情有可矜"的犯人，可被减为流刑、徒刑。"情有可矜"体现了中国古代司法裁判注重情理的特点。

The term means that the circumstances justify leniency. In autumn trials in the Qing Dynasty, the term was used as a verdict for criminals condemned to the death penalty where there were circumstances warranting the commuting of their sentences. It was also referred to as "forgivable," "doubtful" or "dubious circumstances." Cases attracting such judgment were often those involving crimes by the elderly, minors, the disabled and the sick, or homicide to prevent injury to one's parents. Criminals awarded such a verdict might have their sentences reduced to banishment or imprisonment. "Forgivable in view of the circumstances" reflects the priority given to compassion and reason in ancient Chinese judicial decisions.

引例 Citation:

◎ 可矜可疑，情有可矜，事有可疑，仍须审详再定者也。(《六部成语注解·刑部》)

（可被宽恕、存有疑问，即案件依情理可被宽恕，事件的真实情况存有疑问，此类案件的处理办法仍然必须在经过详细审理之后才能确定。）

Forgivable and questionable cases refer to those where the criminals are justifiably forgivable, or the true circumstances are doubtful. Those cases must be handled with detailed hearing. (*Qing Administrative Terminology of the Six Ministries with Explanatory Notes*) shāngyāngfāngshēng

商鞅方升

Fangsheng of Shang Yang

战国时秦国标准量器。商鞅变法时，为统一度量衡而监制的标准量器，又名"商鞅量"。传世的商鞅方升出土于晚清时期。方升为铜质，呈长方形，一侧有柄，其余三个侧面与底部都刻有铭文。底部铭文表明，秦统一六国后，以商鞅确定的度量衡制推行全国。商鞅方升是目前所留存的商鞅变法唯一实物，具有较高的传统法治文化价值。

Fangsheng was a standard measuring vessel of Qin during the Warring States Period. Also known as the "Shang Yang Measure", it was made during the Reforms of Shang Yang to standardize weights and measures. The measuring vessel was unearthed in the late Qing Dynasty. It was made of bronze, rectangular in shape, with a handle on one side and inscriptions on the other three sides and the bottom. The bottom inscription indicates that the system of weights and measures established by Shang Yang was used throughout the country after the State of Qin unified China. As the only existing artefact of the Reforms of Shang Yang, it is of high legal and cultural value.

引例 Citation:

◎ 一法度衡石丈尺。车同轨。书同文字。(《史记·秦始皇本纪》)

（统一法令和度量衡标准。统一车辆两轮间的宽度。书写用同一种文字。）

Standardization of decrees as well as the unit of weights and measures. Standardization of the width between the wheels of carriages and the script for writing. (*Records of the Historian*)

《Shéyù Guījiàn》

《折狱龟鉴》

Sheyu Guijian (*The Reference for Deciding Cases*)

又名《决狱龟鉴》。作者是宋代的郑克。该书分释冤、辨诬、鞫情、议罪、宥过、惩恶、察奸、核奸、察贼、迹贼、严明、矜谨等20门，辑录了上至春秋、下至北宋有关平反冤案、断狱量刑的大量案例。作者对其中大部分内容用按语的方式做了分析和考辨。此书系统地总结了前人在案件侦破、检验、审讯、判决和平反等方面所积累的经验，至今仍具有较高的学术价值，对后世通俗文学也有一定影响。

Also known as *Jueyu Guijian*, this book was written by Zheng Ke of the Song Dynasty. It is divided into 20 subjects, including remedy of injustice, differentiation of false accusations, investigation of cases, deliberation of crimes, forgivable cases, punishment of vice, review of treachery, examination of robbery, tracing of robbers, rigor and honesty, and compassion. It contains a large number of cases relating to the redress of injustice and the determination of sentences from the Spring and Autumn Period to the Northern Song Dynasty, mostly complete with the author's comments. Systematically summarizing the experience of preceding generations in solving and examining cases, questioning suspects, making verdicts and vindicating judgments, it has high academic value and has had an influence on later popular literature.

引例 Citation:

◎ 高宗绍兴三年，降诏恤刑，戒饬中外，俾务哀矜。……（克）因阅和凝《疑狱集》，嘉其用心，乃分类其事……易旧名曰《折狱龟鉴》。"（刘埙《隐居通议》）

(宋高宗绍兴三年（1133年），皇帝下诏书慎用刑法，告诫官员，务必哀怜（百姓）。……（郑克）读到和凝写的《疑狱集》，赞赏他的用心，于是对案例进行分类……把原来的书名改为《折狱龟鉴》。)

In the third year of Shaoxing during the reign of Emperor Gaozong of the Song Dynasty (1133), the emperor issued an imperial edict, requesting caution and mercy in applying the criminal law. ...Zheng Ke appreciated He Ning's intention in reading his *Doubtful Cases*, so he classified the cases in his own book and ... changed the original title to *Sheyu Guijian*. (Liu Xun: *General Discussion on Ancient Texts from a Recluse*) shēnmíngtíng

申明亭

Shenming Pavilion (Declaring Pavilion)

明清时期建于乡邑的教化场所。相传由明太祖朱元璋创建。他命乡邑皆置申明亭，各地耆老（即德高望重老人）、里长（主要掌管户口和纳税的基层官员）在亭内宣读法律文件，受理民间词状，记录官民恶行，以惩恶扬善。明清两代都对申明亭予以法律保护。申明亭制度是明清时期地方治理的重要手段之一，它所体现出来的普及法令、注重道德教化和通过民间调解解决基层纠纷的思路至今仍然有可借鉴之处。

Shenming pavilions were publicity sites built in townships during the Ming and Qing dynasties. Those sites are said to be the invention of Zhu Yuanzhang, the founder of the Ming Dynasty. He ordered all villages and counties to set up such a pavilion, where highly respected elders and grassroots officials mainly in charge of household registry and taxes read out legal documents, addressed complaints from the people, and recorded evil deeds of officials and the people in order to discourage vice and encourage virtue. In the Ming and Qing dynasties, the pavilions were under legal protection. Back then, system was one of the most important means of local governance, and its ideas of popularizing the law, highlighting moral education and settling disputes at the grassroots level through civil mediation are still referential today.

引例 Citation:

◎ 尤择一醇谨端亮者为之，以年则老，识则老，而谙练时务则又老。有渠人因搆（gòu）一亭，书之曰"申明亭"，朔望登之，以从事焉。（海瑞《备忘集》卷六）

（要选择淳厚谨慎、端正诚实的人来担任，原因在于年长的人见多识广、熟悉时务。于是有人搭建了一座亭子，取名为"申明亭"，农历每月初一和十五登临此亭，来执行这项事务。）

The reason for choosing sincere, prudent and honest elders for the post was that they tended to be more knowledgeable and familiar with practical affairs. Therefore, a pavilion was built, called *Shenming* Pavilion. The publicity affair was handled there on the first and fifteenth day of each month in the lunar calendar. (Hai Rui: *Collected Works of Hai Rui*) shéngzhīyǐfǎ

绳之以法

Bring to Justice

依法律制裁犯罪行为。绳，即准绳，木工用的墨线，校正曲直的工具，引申为制裁。在现代社会，"绳之以法"多用于描述依法律办事，惩治犯罪行为，以维护社会安定，实现司法公正。

The term means holding criminals accountable according to law. In the Chinese expression, "绳" means the carpenter's chalk line, which is used as a straightening tool, and figuratively, punishment. In modern society, the phrase "bring to justice" mostly means punishing criminal acts in accordance with law, so as to maintain social stability and judicial fairness.

引例 Citation:

◎ 以文帝之明，而魏尚之忠，绳之以法则为罪，施之以德则为功。(《后汉书·冯衍传》)

（凭着文帝的圣明和魏尚的忠心，文帝依法制裁他（魏尚），他就有罪；文帝对他（魏尚）施加恩德，他就有功。）

By virtue of Emperor Wen's sagacity and Wei Shang's loyalty, Wei would be guilty if Emperor Wen chose to punish him according to law. He would be meritorious by the grace of Emperor Wen. (*History of the Later Han Dynasty*)

shuìhǔdì qínmù zhújiǎn
睡虎地秦墓竹简
Bamboo Slips from Qin Tombs in Shuihudi

湖北云梦睡虎地出土的秦墓竹简。1975年底至1976年初，考古工作者在睡虎地发掘十二座战国墓葬。其中十一号墓出土一批秦代竹简，经整理拼复，共有1155支，另有80片残片，竹简因出土地而得名。从睡虎地秦墓竹简可以看出，自商鞅变法到秦始皇统一六国之前秦国的法制建设之状况。睡虎地秦墓竹简中不仅有刑法，还包括行政法、民法、经济法、诉讼法及军事法等内容。秦始皇正是依靠如此完备的法律体系，才得以完成统一大业，建立起中央集权帝国。睡虎地秦墓竹简对研究古代法制史具有十分重要的价值。

The term refers to bamboo slips discovered in tombs at Shuihudi in Yunmeng, Hubei, China. Archaeologists excavated 12 tombs of the Warring States Period at Shuihudi from late 1975 to early 1976. Among them, Tomb No. 11 yielded a batch of bamboo slips, including 1155 complete ones, and 80 fragments. From the texts on those bamboo slips, we can discern the general legal system in the State of Qin from the time of the Reforms of Shang Yang to the unification of China by Emperor Qin Shi Huang. They recorded not only criminal law, but also administrative law, civil law, economic law, procedural law and military law. It was with such a complete legal system that Emperor Qin Shi Huang managed to accomplish his epic feat and establish a centralized empire. Those bamboo slips are of great value to research on ancient legal history.

引例 Citation:

◎ 百姓居田舍者毋敢酤（酤）酉（酒），田啬夫、部佐谨禁御之，有不从令者有罪。（《睡虎地秦墓竹简·秦律十八种·田律》）

（不准向住在田舍的农村老百姓卖酒。对于向他们卖酒的行为，乡长和部下应该严格禁止，不服从法令的，问罪。）

It is forbidden to sell liquor to rural citizens. The township head and his deputies should strictly prohibit such deeds and hold the offenders accountable. (*Bamboo Slips from Qin Tombs in Shuihudi*) sòngshī mìběn

讼师秘本

Private Books on the Legal Pettifogger System

以教人诉讼为内容的古籍。讼师，即以协助别人进行词讼为业的人。在古代，讼师被官方视为唆使他人无端兴讼之人，受到各级衙门管制。讼师秘本也因被认为是造成"好讼""健讼"的源头而受到统治者的查禁销毁。讼师秘本的流传由此从公开转入暗中。因为它们是向民众普及法律知识的重要途径，所以体现出顽强的生命力和实用价值。

The term refers to ancient books intended to tell people how to proceed with litigation. Pettifoggers were those engaged in assisting others in litigation. In ancient times, they were regarded by the authorities as instigators of unwarranted litigation and controlled by the government at all levels. Private books on the legal pettifogger system were also banned and destroyed by rulers for being the source of "obsession with litigation" and "excessive litigation." Their circulation thus shifted underground. As an important means of spreading legal knowledge, they had strong resilience and practical value.

引例 Citation:

◎ 坊肆所刊讼师秘本，如《惊天雷》《相角》《法家新书》《刑台秦镜》等，一切构讼之书，尽行查禁销毁，不许售卖。(《大清律例·刑律》)

（书坊刊印的讼师秘本，比如《惊天雷》《相角》《法家新书》《刑台秦镜》等，所有这些将会造成诉讼的书，都应该被查禁销毁，不许售卖。）

Private books on the legal pettifogger system, including *Thunder Cracker, Phase Angle, New Book of Legalism,* and *Mirror on Penal Cases*, are all likely to stir litigation, and thus should be censored, destroyed, and prohibited from selling. (*The Qing Code*)

《Tángliùdiǎn》

《唐六典》

The Six Statutes of the Tang Dynasty

又名《大唐六典》。原题唐玄宗御撰，李林甫奉敕注。《唐六典》是一部以唐代开元年间职官制度为本，追溯其历代沿革源流，以明设官分职之义的考典之书。依照唐玄宗本意，此书应按《周官》分六部分，故称《唐六典》。但是，由于唐代官制与周代相差较大，《唐六典》仍按唐代国家机关实际情况进行编撰。《唐六典》规定了唐代中央和地方国家机关的机构、编制、职责、人员、品位、待遇等，注中又叙述了官制的历史沿革。有论者将它视为中国古代具有行政法典性质的官修书。

Also known as *The Six Statutes of the Great Tang Dynasty*, the code had a title originally inscribed by Emperor Xuanzong of the Tang Dynasty, and annotations made by Li Linfu according to imperial decree. It traced the history of the official system during the Kaiyuan Reign in the Tang Dynasty, and clarified the establishment of official posts and the division of duties. Emperor Xuanzong originally intended to have it divided into six parts according to *Official Titles of Zhou*, hence the name "The Six Statutes of the Tang Dynasty." However, as the official system of the Tang Dynasty differed considerably from that of the Zhou Dynasty, it was still compiled according to the actual establishment of state agencies. It set out the institutions, establishment, duties, personnel, ranking and salaries of the central and local state authorities of the Tang Dynasty, with the historical evolution of the official system in the annotations. Some commentators regard it as an official revision of the administrative code in ancient China.

引例 Citation:

◎ 唐、虞而下，损益沿革咸具焉。昔宋祁论唐制精密简要；曾巩谓《六典》得建官制理之方，文不烦而实备。（王鏊《震泽集·重刊〈唐六典〉序》）

（尧舜以来，（行政制度的）增删、继承和变化都出现了。从前宋祁曾论述唐代的制度精密简要，曾巩说《唐六典》对设置官职、治理国家的阐述得当，文字言简意赅。）

Since Emperor Yao and Shun, we have made additions, deletions, successions and changes to the administrative system. Previously, Song Qi discussed the precision and brevity of the system in the Tang Dynasty. Zeng Gong said that *The Six Statutes of the Tang Dynasty,* with concise texts, was a good exposition on the establishment of official positions and governance of the state. (Wang Ao: *Collected Works of Wang Ao*)

《Tánglǜ Shūyì》

《唐律疏议》

Commentary on the Tang Code

又名《永徽律疏》。唐高宗永徽元年（650年），长孙无忌等人奉诏在武德、贞观两律的基础上修订新律，次年完成，即《永徽律》。三年五月，高宗又诏长孙无忌等人为律作疏，旨在说明历史沿革和解释词义法理，于四年十一月撰成，即《永徽律疏》。《唐律疏议》包括律文和疏议两部分，律文《永徽律》是法律条文，疏议是对律文的解释，与律文具有同等效力。《唐律疏议》共三十卷、十二篇、五百零二条。《唐律疏议》不但是中国古代法典的杰出代表，也深深影响了东亚各国的古代立法实践。

The *Commentary on the Tang Code* is also known as the *Yonghui Code with Annotations*. In the first year of Yonghui (650), Zhangsun Wuji and his team were ordered to formulate a new law based on the laws of the Wude Reign and the Zhenguan Reign. The project was completed in the following year, and the result was known as the *Yonghui Code*. In the fifth month of the third year, Emperor Gaozong again ordered Zhangsun Wuji and his team to make annotations of the law, to explain the historical development and the meaning of the terms. The annotation was completed in the eleventh month of the fourth year, and the result was known as the *Commentary on the Tang Code*. It consists of two parts: legal texts and discussions. The legal texts are provisions in *Yonghui Code* and the discussions are their interpretation, which has the same effect. *Commentary on the Tang Code* consists of 502 articles in 30 volumes, and in 12 parts. As an outstanding example of the ancient Chinese legal codes, it has deeply influenced the ancient legislative practices of East Asian countries.

引例 Citation:

◎ 唐律一准乎礼，以为出入得古今之平。(《四库全书总目提要》卷八十二)
　　(唐律以儒家的礼为立法标准，刑制平缓，轻重适中，是古往今来最公平的法律。)

The *Tang Code* was legislated on the basis of Confucian rites. With mild and moderate penalties, it is the fairest law of all times. (*Catalogue of the Complete Library of the Four Branches of Literature*) tóngguǐ

铜匦

The Bronze Suggestion Box

　　唐代武则天时期置于内廷的铜制匣子。铜匦是武则天所创，用来随时接受天下表疏，类似于现代的"意见箱"。铜匦在东、南、西、北四面各设一个格门，以便官吏、百姓将申冤、告密、进谏、颂扬等不同性质的信函分别投入其中。匦由专职官员管理，以确保言路畅通，下情上达。铜匦制度开辟了一条最高统治者了解下情的渠道。但是，铜匦后来逐渐沦为酷吏政治中的"举报箱"，成为武则天时期告密之风盛行的缩影。

The term refers to a bronze box placed in the inner court during the reign of Empress Wu Zetian of the Tang Dynasty. Similar to the modern "suggestion box," it was created by Wu Zetian to receive memorials from the people. It had one latticed door on the east, south, west, and north respectively for officials and ordinary people to put letters of different natures, for the redress of injustices, denunciation, advice, and praise. An official was specifically charged with managing the box to ensure smooth communication and the dissemination of information. The system opened up a channel for the supreme ruler to learn about public opinion. However, the box was gradually reduced to a "report box" in the political maneuvering of merciless officials, and became an epitome of prevalent snitching during the reign of Empress Wu Zetian.

引例 Citation:

◎ 则天临朝，初欲大收人望。垂拱初年，令熔铜为匦，四面置门，各依方色，共为一室。(《旧唐书·刑法志》)

(武则天临朝，起初想大收人望。垂拱初年，命人熔铜铸成匦，四面设门，各依四方的颜色，合起来成为一室。）

When Wu Zetian first took over the anvil, she hoped to gain support from the people. Therefore, she ordered to have a bronze box cast, with a door on each of the four sides, having a color depending on its direction. The four doors were assembled around one chamber. (*The Old Tang History*) wǎngkāi-yīmiàn

网开一面

Give Wrongdoers a Leeway

把猎网打开一面，给鸟兽留下逃生的道路。比喻在适用法律时采取宽大态度，给罪犯一条弃旧从新的出路。原作"网开三面"。"网开一面"俗语体现了中国人在适用规则时兼顾情理的思维习惯。

The concept literally means opening the net on one side to leave a way for birds and beasts to escape. It is a metaphor for leniency in the application of law, so as to give criminals a second chance. Preceded by an expression meaning "opening the net on three sides" in Chinese, it embodies the Chinese habit of considering both laws and compassion in applying rules.

引例 Citation:

◎ 汤出，见野张网四面，祝曰："自天下四方，皆入吾网。"汤曰："嘻，尽之矣！"乃去其三面。(《史记·殷本纪》)

（商王成汤外出，看见有人在野外把四面都张满了网，并祷告说："天下四方的鸟兽，都到我的网里来。"汤说："哎呀，这样（太残忍了，）把鸟兽都捕光了。"于是把网收起了三面。）

King Cheng Tang of the Shang Dynasty saw a man spreading a net on all sides in the field and praying "May all animals from far and wide come into my net." He said, "Alas! That is too cruel; you are going to kill all the birds and beasts." Therefore, he removed the net on three sides. (*Records of the Historian*) xièzhì

獬豸

Xiezhi

　　古代传说中的神兽，能辨别是非曲直。大者如牛，小者如羊，长相类似麒麟，通体黑色毛发，双眼明亮有神，额上有一角。獬豸见人争斗时，会以独角顶理亏之人。相传，皋陶被虞舜任命为法官后，审判疑案多用獬豸，以明是非。古汉字"灋"（fǎ）结构中的"廌"（zhì）便是指獬豸，取其公正之意。至今，獬豸的形象仍是中国法院、律师事务所、法学院等场所常用的标志。

Xiezhi was a legendary mythical ancient creature with the born ability to distinguish right from wrong. The large ones could reach the size of an ox, while the small ones were the size of a goat. It resembled *qilin*, but had dark fur, bright eyes and a single horn on its forehead. When hearing an argument, it would ram the wrongful party with its horn. According to legend, it was frequently used by Gao Yao, a judge appointed by Emperor Shun, to tell right from wrong when hearing disputed cases. The component "廌" in "灋", the ancient form of the Chinese character for law, refers to *xiezhi*, for its connotation of "justice." Today, *xiezhi* is still a common symbol used by courts, law firms, and law schools in China.

　　引例 Citation:

◎ 獬豸，神羊，能别曲直，楚王尝获之，故以为冠。（《后汉书·舆服志下》）

　　（獬豸，一种神羊，能够辨别是非曲直。楚王曾经捕获过獬豸，照其形制成帽子。）

Xiezhi is a mythical goat with an innate ability to distinguish right from wrong. The King of Chu once caught one and made a hat decorated with its image. (*History of the Later Han Dynasty*) xíngdǐng

刑鼎

Penal Pot

古代铸有刑法条文的铜鼎。"刑"指法律条文。"鼎"指古代供烹煮用的器物，也是一种贵族用的礼器。春秋后期"铸刑鼎"，通常被认为是古代公布成文法的开端。根据史书记载，"铸刑鼎"出现过两次：一次出现在郑国，周景王九年（前536年），子产把法律条文刻铸在鼎上；一次出现在晋国，周敬王七年（前513年），赵鞅和荀寅把范宣子制定的法律刻铸于鼎。这种将法律公布于众的做法标志着中国古代法律从"秘密法"演变至"公布法"，具有进步意义。秦代以后，刑律多刻写于竹简或草纸上，故不再"铸刑鼎"。

Known as *xingding* in ancient China, penal pots are ancient bronze tripods engraved with the criminal law provisions. *Xing* refers to the provisions of law, while *ding* refers to ancient cooking vessels, which were also ceremonial vessels used by the nobility. "Casting penal pots" in the late Spring and Autumn Period is often considered the beginning of the promulgation of written law in ancient times. According to historical records, there were two instances of "casting penal pots." One was in the State of Zheng, in the ninth year of King Jing of Zhou (536 BC), when Zichan engraved legal provisions on a tripod. The other occurred in the State of Jin, in the seventh year of King Jing of Zhou (513 BC), when Zhao Yang and Xun Yin engraved the laws laid down by Fanxuanzi on a tripod. This practice of making the laws public marked the progressive evolution of ancient Chinese law from "secret law" to "publicized law." After the Qin Dynasty, most of the criminal laws were carved on bamboo slips or written on straw paper. Consequently, the practice of "casting penal pots" was abolished.

引例 Citation:

◎ 冬，晋赵鞅、荀寅帅师城汝滨，遂赋晋国一鼓铁，以铸刑鼎，著范宣子所为刑书焉。(《左传·昭公二十九年》)

（冬，晋赵鞅、荀寅率领军队在汝水边筑城，就向晋国人民征收了四百八十斤铁，用来铸造刑鼎，铸上范宣子所制定的刑法。）

In winter, when Zhao Yang and Xun Yin from the State of Jin led troops to build a city by the Rushui River, they levied 480 catties of iron from the locals to cast a penal pot, and had the criminal law formulated by Fanxuanzi engraved upon it. (*Zuo's Commentary on The Spring and Autumn Annals*) yámen

衙门

Yamen

古代称官府为衙门。"衙门"由"牙门"转化而来。"牙门"本指军旅营门，因营门两侧常用木头刻画猛兽利牙来象征勇武而得名。称官府为衙门也是为了体现权力的威严。官府称衙门始于唐，盛于宋，沿用至明清，距今已有一千多年的历史。在古代，上至皇帝属下各部，下至地方州县官府，都可称作衙门。在老百姓眼中，衙门一般是指和自身关系密切的州县官府。州县衙门职能广泛，综合管理辖区内各项事务。

Yamen (衙门) was the administrative office of a local mandarin in ancient China. Originally, it was derived from the homonym *yamen* (牙门), a gate used for military camps or establishments. On each side of the gate, a wooden post carved with the teeth of fierce beasts was erected, as a symbol of bravery. In the Tang Dynasty, administrative offices began to be called *yamen* to show the authority of power. The practice became prevalent in the Song Dynasty, and extended to the Ming and Qing dynasties, having a history of more than a thousand years. In ancient times, *yamen* was the name of government offices from the central ministries down to the local counties and prefectures. For ordinary people, it generally referred to the local county government closely related to their life. The *yamen* of prefectures and counties usually served a wide range of functions and managed various affairs within its jurisdiction.

引例 Citation:

◎ 每日衙门虚寂，无复诉讼者。(《北齐书·宋世良传》)

（每天衙门空无一人，再没有来打官司的。）

Every day, the *yamen* was deserted and no one came here for litigation. (*The History of the Northern Qi Dynasty*) yǒulǐchéng

羑里城

Youli City

中国历史上有文字记载的第一座国家监狱。羑里城是周文王姬昌被商纣王囚禁而推演《周易》的地方。遗址位于今河南安阳汤阴县城北四公里处。商代末期，姬昌势力逐渐增大，纣王怀疑他谋反，便将之囚禁于此。姬昌发愤图强，在此推演《周易》。历史上，人们曾多次在此修建纪念周文王的庙宇。

Youli City is the first recorded state prison in Chinese history. It was the place where Ji Chang, King Wen of the vassal state Zhou, was imprisoned by King Zhou of the Shang Dynasty and where he formulated *The Book of Changes*. Its ruins are located four kilometers north of present-day Tangyin, Anyang, Henan Province. At the end of the Shang Dynasty, Ji Chang grew increasingly powerful, and King Zhou suspected him of plotting a rebellion and imprisoned him there. Ji Chang strived against the adversity and deduced *The Book of Changes* there. Historically, many temples were built there to commemorate him.

引例 Citation:

◎ 西伯昌闻之，窃叹，崇侯虎知之，以告纣，纣囚西伯羑里。(《史记·殷本纪》)

（西伯昌听到这件事，暗暗叹息。崇侯虎得知后，去向纣王告发，纣王把西伯昌囚禁在羑里。）

Ji Chang secretly sighed after hearing about the event. But Hu, the Duke of Chong, reported the incident to King Zhou, who imprisoned Ji Chang in Youli. (*Records of the Historian*) yìngyí

㒕匜

Yingyi

㒕匜是西周青铜器之名。㒕，人名。匜，礼器名。1975年出土于陕西岐山。长椭圆形，四足为羊蹄，配有琵琶形的兽头盖子。器盖和腹底内壁上刻有铭文，记载的是迄今所见最早的诉讼判决书，记叙了西周时期一起奴隶买卖纠纷的经过，具有很高的史料价值，对于研究西周法律制度有极为重要的意义。

Yingyi is the name of a bronze of the Western Zhou Dynasty. *Ying* is the name of a person, and *yi* is the name of a ritual bronze. Excavated from Qishan, Shaanxi in 1975, the oblong bronze had four legs shaped after goat feet and a lid shaped after the Chinese lute and featuring a beast head. The inscriptions on the lid and the interior of the bottom bear the earliest litigation judgment ever seen, recording the settlement of a dispute over a sale of slaves in the Western Zhou Dynasty. It has great value as a historical record and is of great importance for studying the legal system of the Western Zhou Dynasty.

引例 Citation:

◎ 白扬父廼（nǎi）成𣪘（hài），曰："牧牛！徂乃可湛。女敢以乃师讼……罚女三百寽（lüè）。"白扬父廼或吏牧牛誓曰："自今余敢扰乃小大史。"……牧牛辞誓成，罚金。㒕用乍旅盉（hé）。（秦永龙《西周金文选注》）

（司法官伯扬父判决说："牧牛！之前你的行为何其过分。你竟敢与你的上司㒕打官司……罚你缴纳铜三百寽。"伯扬父又让牧牛发誓说：" 从今以后，我大事小事再也不敢扰乱你了。" ……牧牛的书面誓词写成了，罚金也交上来了。䙄用这铜做成了旅盉。）

Judge Boyangfu made a judgment, saying, "Muniu! Your previous behavior was so egregious. How dare you file a lawsuit against Ying, your superior... You are sentenced to a fine of 300 *lüe of* copper." He then asked the latter to swear that he would refrain from disturbing his superior, for whatever reason... Soon, the pledge was finished in writing and the fine was paid. Ying turned the copper into a wine vessel. (Qin Yonglong: *Selected and Annotated Chinese Bronze Inscriptions of the Western Zhou Dynasty*) zhāngjiāshān hànmù zhújiǎn

张家山汉墓竹简

Bamboo Slips from Han Tombs in Zhangjiashan

1983年在湖北江陵（今荆州）城外西南约15公里的张家山出土的西汉时期竹简，对中国法律史研究意义重大。内容丰富，包括《二年律令》《奏谳书》等八种文献。《二年律令》的发现使亡佚已久的汉律得以重现，成为系统研究古代法律的最直接史料。《奏谳书》是秦、汉司法诉讼制度的直接记录，从中可以了解该时期法律实施状况。

The bamboo slips of the Western Han Dynasty unearthed in 1983 in Zhangjiashan, about 15 kilometers southwest of Jiangling (now Jingzhou), Hubei Province, are of great significance for studying Chinese legal history. They are rich in content, and are comprised of eight documents, including *The Code of the Second Year of Empress Lü Zhi*, and *The Book of Submitted Doubtful Cases*. The discovery of *The Code of the Second Year of Empress Lü Zhi* has made it possible to recover the long-lost laws of the Han Dynasty, furnishing direct historical material for the systematic study of ancient laws. *The Book of Submitted Doubtful Cases* is a direct record of the judicial system of the Qin and Han dynasties, making possible an understanding of law enforcement back then.

引例 Citation:

◎ 贩卖缯布幅不盈二尺二寸者，没入之。能捕告者，以畀之。(《张家山汉墓竹简·二年律令》)

（贩卖布匹的幅度不足二尺二寸的，由官府没收。经人举报查实的，赠送给举报人。）

Cloth for sale that is under two feet and two inches in width shall be confiscated by the government, and given to the informant for free, if his information has led to the confiscation. (*Bamboo Slips from Han Tombs in Zhangjiashan*) zhífǎ-rúshān

执法如山

Enforce the Law Unwaveringly

执行法律应坚定如山，毫不动摇。相传唐代雍州司户李元纮，在上司因畏惧强权而改判时，挥笔在原判决书的空白之处书写"南山可移，此判无动"八个大字，维持了正义。后人将这八个字浓缩成"执法如山"。史书中有许多中国古代严格执法、不徇私情的事例。狄仁杰、包拯、海瑞等富有传奇色彩的古代官员正是典型。至今，"执法如山"仍时刻提醒着当下法律人执行法律应坚定不移。

The enforcement of the law should be firm and unwavering. According to legend, Li Yuanhong, an official of Yongzhou in the Tang Dynasty, maintained justice by writing on the margin of his verdict eight Chinese characters meaning "The South Mountain may be moved, but not this judgment" when his superiors tried to overturn it due to fear of power. Later generations condensed his words into the phrase "enforce the law unwaveringly." In history books, there are many records of strict law enforcement without favoritism. Legendary officials such as Di Renjie, Bao Zheng and Hai Rui are typical examples. In modern times, the term is still a constant reminder for legal professionals to uphold the law with resolution.

引例 Citation:

◎ 言出如箭，执法如山。（李绿园《歧路灯》第八十八回）
（说出来的话像放出去的箭一样，执行法律法令像大山屹立一样坚决不动摇。）

Uttered words are like released arrows. Enforcement of laws and decrees should be as resolute and unshakeable as a great mountain. (Li Lüyuan: *Lamp of the Forked Road*) zhíshì

执事

Zhishi

"执事"一词有多种含义，在传统法治文化史上指在衙门公案左右各列的写有"肃静""回避"的牌子、官员职衔牌以及军杖等器物，其功能在于强化自身权威。这些器物在民间戏曲、民俗活动、通俗小说中被加以借用和演绎，成为传统法治文化中独具特色的部分。

This term has various meanings. In the history of legal culture, it referred to plaques carrying words meaning "Silence" and "Keep clear," as well as official title plates, and staffs placed next to the desk of government offices. As legal objects used in government offices in ancient times to reinforce authority, they were depicted in folk operas, folk customs and popular novels, to become a distinctive part of traditional Chinese rule of law culture.

引例 Citation:

◎ 当下定了主意，次早传齐轿夫，也不用全副执事，只带八个红黑帽夜役军牢。翟买办扶着轿子，一直下乡来。（吴敬梓《儒林外史》第一回）

The magistrate made up his mind. The next morning, he assembled the bearers and refused all fanfare, bringing with him only eight runners. This way he came straight to the countryside in a sedan, with Comprador Zhai waiting on him. (Wu Jingzi: *The Scholars*)

术语表 List of Concepts

中文	英文	页码
安人宁国	Providing Peace and Comfort to the People and Keeping the State at Peace	003
别籍异财	Separate Wealth and Separate Household	061
差官别推	Transfer to Higher Authority for Retrial	062
春秋决狱	Adjudicating Cases According to Doctrines in *The Spring and Autumn Annals*	005
存留养亲	Permitting a Criminal to Support Lineal Elders	064
大理寺	*Dalisi* (The Court of Judicial Review)	066
德本刑用	Morality as the Foundation and Penalty as the Means	007
德主刑辅	Morality Given Priority over Penalty	008
登闻鼓	*Dengwen* Drum	119
罚当其罪	Punishment Commensurate with the Crime	010
法必明，令必行	The Laws Shall Be Just and Impartial and the Promulgated Acts Shall Be Enforced.	011
法不阿贵	The Law Does Not Favor the Rich and the Powerful.	012
法贵简当	Enacting Concise and Reasonable Laws	013
《法经》	*Canon of Laws*	121
法令滋彰，盗贼多有	The More Laws and Orders Are Made Prominent, the More Thieves and Robbers There Will Be.	015
法深无善治	Too Stringent and Too Many Laws Prevent Good Governance.	017
法与时转则治	Laws in Line with the Times Produce Good Governance.	018
翻异别勘	*Fanyi Biekan* (Retrial Regarding Overturned Confession)	068
诽谤木	*Feibangmu* (Commentary Column)	123

177

中文	英文	页码
奉法者强则国强	Strong Conformers to the Law Make the Country Strong.	019
符牌	Tally	124
告状/诉状	*Gaozhuang/Suzhuang* (Pleadings)	126
格	*Ge* (Ruling)	070
公案小说	Public-case Novel	127
官联	Official Couplet	129
官清法正	Clean and Honest Officials for Fair Law Enforcement	130
规矩	*Guiju* (Rules and Norms)	132
和为贵	Harmony Is Most Precious.	020
虎符	Tiger Tally	133
化外人相犯	Crime Among Foreign Persons	072
换推	Withdrawal and Reelection	074
戒石坊	*Jieshifang* (Admonition Archway)	135
矜老恤幼	Reduction or Exemption of Criminal Responsibility in Minors and the Elderly	075
进善旌	Banner for Advice	137
经国序民，正其制度	Creating an Orderly Society When Governing a Country Requires Improved Systems.	022
惊堂木	The Chinese Gavel	138
九卿会审	Joint Hearing by the Nine Ministers	076
鞫谳分司	Separation of *Ju* and *Yan*	078
举轻以明重，举重以明轻	Illustrating the Heavy with the Light, and the Light with the Heavy	080

中文	英文	页码
礼不下庶人，刑不上大夫	Rites Do Not Extend Down to the Common People and Criminal Punishment Does Not Extend Up to the Senior Nobles.	023
礼法合一	Unification of Rites and Laws	024
礼乐不兴，则刑罚不中	If Rituals and Music Do Not Flourish, Punishments Will Not Be Meted out Properly.	026
令	*Ling* (Ordinance)	082
令签	*Lingqian*	139
六礼	Six-procedure Marriage Rite	083
录囚	Investigating Prisoners	085
律	*Lü* (Statute)	086
民惟邦本	People Are the Foundation of the State.	028
明德慎罚	The Illustration of Virtue and the Cautious Use of Punishments	029
明镜高悬	Bright Mirror Hung High	141
明刑弼教	Making Penalties Explicit to Assist Moral Education	031
墨者之法	Mohist Law	087
契约	Contract	142
亲亲相隐	Relatives Mutually Conceal Their Misconduct.	032
情有可矜	Forgivable in View of the Circumstances	144
秋冬行刑	Execution of Sentences in Autumn and Winter	089
秋审	Autumn Trial	091
仁义之法	The Standards of Benevolence and Righteousness	033
任德不任刑	Morality-ruling over Penalty-ruling	034
三刺之法	Three Interrogations	093

179

中文	英文	页码
三司推事	Joint Trial by Three Departments	094
三宥三赦	Leniency for Three Kinds of Criminal Circumstances and Pardon for Three Kinds of Criminals	036
商鞅方升	*Fangsheng* of Shang Yang	146
《折狱龟鉴》	*Sheyu Guijian* (*The Reference for Deciding Cases*)	147
申明亭	*Shenming* Pavilion (Declaring Pavilion)	149
慎刑	Prudential Punishment	038
绳之以法	Bring to Justice	151
十恶不赦	Ten Unpardonable Abominations	096
式	*Shi* (Models)	098
睡虎地秦墓竹简	Bamboo Slips from Qin Tombs in Shuihudi	152
讼师秘本	Private Books on the Legal Pettifogger System	154
《唐六典》	*The Six Statutes of the Tang Dynasty*	156
《唐律疏议》	*Commentary on the Tang Code*	158
天理、国法、人情	Heavenly Principle, State Law, and Human Nature	040
天人合一	Heaven and Man Are United as One.	100
天网恢恢，疏而不漏	Justice Has Long Arms.	041
天下之法	Universal Law	042
铜匦	The Bronze Suggestion Box	160
徒法不足以自行	Laws Alone Cannot Carry Themselves into Practice.	044
王子犯法，与庶民同罪	All Offenders Shall Be Punished by Law Equally, Be They Princes or Commoners.	045

中文	英文	页码
网开一面	Give Wrongdoers a Leeway	162
为政以德	Governance Based on Virtue	046
无讼	(A Society) Free from Litigation	047
五覆奏	Five Rounds of Reassessment of Death Sentences	102
息讼	Quell Litigation	048
獬豸	*Xiezhi*	163
刑	*Xing*	103
刑部	The Ministry of Justice	104
刑鼎	Penal Pot	165
刑名幕友	*Xingming Muyou* (Legal Advisors)	106
刑无等级	Punishments Should Know No Degree or Grade.	050
恤刑	Penalty with Prudence	107
衙门	*Yamen*	167
一断于法	Judging All by Law	052
偾匦	*Yingyi*	170
移司别勘	Internal Transfer for Retrial	108
有治法而后有治人	Talents of Governance Appear After Good Laws Are Made.	053
羑里城	Youli City	169
御史台	The Censorate	110
约法三章	Three Regulations	112
张家山汉墓竹简	Bamboo Slips from Han Tombs in Zhangjiashan	172
执法如山	Enforce the Law Unwaveringly	174
执事	*Zhishi*	176

181

中文	英文	页码
治国无其法则乱，守法而不变则衰	Ruling a Country Without Laws Brings Chaos While Rigidly Following Laws Without Reform Leads to Decline.	055
周公制礼	The Duke of Zhou's Establishment of Rites	113
准五服以制罪	Conviction and Punishment Based on *Wufu*	115
罪疑惟轻	Dealing with Doubtful Crimes Lightly	057

参考文献 References

1. 阿风. 中国历史上的"契约"[J]. 安徽史学, 2015（4）: 5—12.
2. 北京大学法学百科全书编委会. 北京大学法学百科全书[Z]. 北京: 北京大学出版社, 2016.
3. 陈鼓应. 老子今注今译[M]. 北京: 商务印书馆, 2003.
4. 陈一石. "礼不下庶人, 刑不上大夫"辨[J]. 法学研究, 1981（1）: 49—53.
5. 程忠学. "明镜高悬"的来历[J]. 咬文嚼字, 1996（11）: 46.
6. 党江舟. 中国传统讼师文化研究[D]. 中国政法大学博士论文, 2003.
7. 邓建鹏. 健讼与息讼——中国传统诉讼文化的矛盾解析[J]. 清华法学, 2004（1）: 176—200.
8. 《法学词典》编辑委员会. 法学词典[Z]. 上海: 上海辞书出版社, 1980.
9. 范忠信, 郑定, 詹学农. 情理法与中国人——中国传统法律文化探微[M]. 北京: 中国人民大学出版社, 1992.
10. 范忠信. 中西法律传统中的"亲亲相隐"[J]. 中国社会科学, 1997（3）: 87—104.
11. 夫马进, 李力. 讼师秘本的世界[J]. 北大法律评论, 2010（1）: 210—238.
12. 巩富文. 唐代的三司推事制[J]. 人文杂志, 1993（4）: 117.
13. 何明. 矜老恤幼思想的历史推进与现代展开[J]. 周口师范学院学报, 2018, 35（3）: 114—117.
14. 黄纯艳. 宋代登闻鼓制度[J]. 中州学刊, 2004（6）: 112—116.
15. 霍存福. 中国古代契约精神的内涵及其现代价值[J]. 吉林大学社会科学学报, 2008（5）: 57—64.
16. 江隐龙. 法律博物馆: 文物中的法律故事[M]. 北京: 中国法制出版社, 2021.
17. 蒋铁初. 中国古代的罪疑惟轻[J]. 法学研究, 2010, 32（2）: 196—208.
18. 金耀基. 中国民本思想史[M]. 北京: 法律出版社, 2008.
19. 李灿. 初论清代刑名幕友[J]. 西南政法大学学报, 2013, 15（5）: 15—21.
20. 李德嘉. "德主刑辅"说的学说史考察[J]. 政法论丛, 2018（2）: 153—160.
21. 李德嘉. 董仲舒"任德不任刑"的思想辨正[J]. 江汉学术, 2017, 36（4）: 97—102.
22. 李交发. 中国诉讼法史[M]. 湘潭: 湘潭大学出版社, 2016.
23. 李勤通. 论礼法融合对唐宋司法制度的影响[J]. 江苏社会科学, 2018, （4）:

142—151.

24. 李文静. 宋代司法审判中的鞠谳分司 [N]. 学习时报，2014-1-20（A9）.
25. 李兴濂. 进善旌·诽谤木·登闻鼓 [J]. 杂文月刊，2014（11）：15.
26. 李学勤. 张家山汉简研究的几个问题 [J]. 郑州大学学报（哲学社会科学版），2002（3）：5—7.
27. 梁涛. "亲亲相隐"与"隐而任之" [J]. 哲学研究，2012（10）：35—42，128.
28. 梁治平."礼法"探原 [J]. 清华法学，2015（1）：81—116.
29. 刘昌安，温勤能. 婚姻"六礼"的文化内涵 [J]. 汉中师院学报（社会科学版），1994，（2）：39—43.
30. 刘春梅. 论明清申明亭的起源、兴废及功用 [J]. 成都师范学院学报，2016（4）：112—115.
31. 刘海年. 㝬匜铭文及其所反映的西周刑制 [J]. 法学研究，1984（1）：81—88.
32. 刘宏，熊丹. 古代死刑复核复奏制度的借鉴意义 [J]. 人民论坛，2011（26）：92—93.
33. 刘瑞明. 古代"官联"拾趣 [J]. 廉政瞭望，2005（7）：58.
34. 刘信芳."礼不下庶人，刑不上大夫"辨疑 [J]. 中国史研究，2004（1）：23—28.
35. 马飞. 以道尊君与诠法——慎到政治哲学再阐释 [J]. 北京行政学院学报，2020（5）：110—117.
36. 马小红，柴荣. 中国法制史 [M]. 北京：北京师范大学出版社，2009.
37. 马小红."一家之法""天下之法"——中国古代的两次法治思潮 [J]. 师大法学，2018（2）：51—68.
38. 马小红. 礼与法：法的历史连接 [M]. 北京：北京大学出版社，2004.
39. 马小红. 释"礼不下庶人，刑不上大夫"[J]. 法学研究，1987（2）：71，83—85.
40. 马小红. 中国法思想史新编 [M]. 南京：南京大学出版社，2015.
41. 马小红. 中国古代法巡礼 [N]. 法制日报，2017-08-16（10）.
42. 马小红等. 中国法律史教程 [M]. 北京：商务印书馆，2020.
43. 乜小红. 中国古代契约发展简史 [M]. 北京：中华书局，2017.
44. 宁志新.《唐六典》仅仅是一般的官修典籍吗?[J]. 中国社会科学，1994（2）：193—196.
45. 蒲坚. 中国法制史大辞典 [Z]. 北京：北京大学出版社，2015.
46. 钱穆. 论语新解 [M]. 武汉：长江文艺出版社，2020.

47. 曲彦斌 . 中国婚礼仪式史略 [J]. 民俗研究，2000（2）：75—88.

48. 施宣圆，等 . 中国文化辞典 [Z]. 上海：上海社会科学院出版社，1987.

49. 睡虎地秦墓竹简整理小组 . 睡虎地秦墓竹简 [M]. 北京：文物出版社，1990.

50. 孙倩 . 论中国古代的罪疑惟轻 [J]. 法制与社会发展，2017，23（2）：26—41.

51. 王春林 . 论中国古代法律中的矜老恤幼原则 [J]. 广西青年干部学院学报，2006（4）：68—69，72.

52. 王国庆 . 品读内乡县衙 [M]. 北京：华艺出版社，2010.

53. 王杰 . 经国序民 正其制度 [N]. 光明日报，2020-01-08（2）.

54. 王捷 ."直诉"源流通说辨正 [J]. 法学研究，2015（6）：174—190.

55. 王俊文 . 古代官联 [J]. 河北企业，2004（4）：33.

56. 王沛 . 刑鼎、宗族法令与成文法公布——以两周铭文为基础的研究 [J]. 中国社会科学，2019（3）：85—105.

57. 王威威 . 韩非思想研究：以黄老为本 [M]. 南京：南京大学出版社，2012.

58. 吴兢 . 贞观政要 [M]. 骈宇骞，骈骅，译 . 北京：中华书局，2009.

59. 武树臣，李力 . 法家思想与法家精神 [M]. 北京：中央广播电视大学出版社，1998.

60. 武树臣 . 中国法律思想史 [M]. 北京：法律出版社，2004.

61. 夏勇 . 民本与民权——中国权利话语的历史基础 [J]. 中国社会科学，2004（5）：4—23，205.

62. 徐进 . 孔子"无讼"辨正 [J]. 齐鲁学刊，1984（4）：40—42，52.

63. 徐忠明 . 凡俗与神圣：解读"明镜高悬"的司法意义 [J]. 中国法学，2010（2）：128—142.

64. 杨宽 . 战国史 [M]. 上海：上海人民出版社，2019.

65. 杨文闯 . 官与官联 [J]. 党风与廉政，1995（9）：1.

66. 杨小军 . 信访法治化改革与完善研究 [J]. 中国法学，2013（5）：22—33.

67. 尤陈俊 . 法律知识的文字传播 [M]. 上海：上海人民出版社，2013.

68. 曾振宇 . 商鞅法哲学研究 [J]. 史学月刊，2000（6）：26—33.

69. 詹奇玮 . 慎刑思想的历史审视与当代提倡——兼论与域外谦抑理念的比较 [J]. 社会科学，2022，（6）：178—191.

70. 张岱年 . 中华思想大辞典 [M]. 长春：吉林人民出版社，1991.

71. 张家山二四七号汉墓竹简整理小组 . 张家山汉墓竹简 [M]. 北京：文物出版社，2006.

72. 张晋藩 . 论中国古代的司法镜鉴 [J]. 政法论坛，2019（3）：3—13.

73. 张军胜. 登闻鼓源流略探 [J]. 青海民族学院学报（社会科学版），2009（3）：78—80.
74. 张雷. 试论我国古代恤刑制度及其历史评价 [D]. 天津师范大学硕士论文，2013.
75. 赵晶.《天圣令》与唐宋法制考论 [M]. 上海：上海古籍出版社，2020.
76. 赵武宏. 细说汉字 [M]. 北京：大众文艺出版社，2010.
77. 赵晓耕，沈玮玮. 专业之作：中国三十年（1979—2009）立法检视 [J]. 辽宁大学学报（哲学社会科学版），2010，38（5）：1—10.
78. 朱腾. 从君主命令到令、律之别——先秦法律形式变迁史纲 [J]. 清华法学，2020，14（02）：157—186.

中国历史年代简表 A Brief Chronology of Chinese History

远古时代 Prehistory			
夏 Xia Dynasty			c. 2070 - 1600 BC
商 Shang Dynasty			1600 - 1046 BC
周 Zhou Dynasty	西周 Western Zhou Dynasty		1046 - 771 BC
	东周 Eastern Zhou Dynasty 　春秋时代 Spring and Autumn Period 　战国时代 Warring States Period		770 - 256 BC 770 - 476 BC 475 - 221 BC
秦 Qin Dynasty			221 - 206 BC
汉 Han Dynasty	西汉 Western Han Dynasty		206 BC-AD 25
	东汉 Eastern Han Dynasty		25 - 220
三国 Three Kingdoms	魏 Kingdom of Wei		220 - 265
	蜀 Kingdom of Shu		221 - 263
	吴 Kingdom of Wu		222 - 280
晋 Jin Dynasty	西晋 Western Jin Dynasty		265 - 317
	东晋 Eastern Jin Dynasty 十六国 Sixteen States*		317 - 420 304 - 439
南北朝 Southern and Northern Dynasties	南朝 Southern Dynasties	宋 Song Dynasty	420 - 479
		齐 Qi Dynasty	479 - 502
		梁 Liang Dynasty	502 - 557
		陈 Chen Dynasty	557 - 589
	北朝 Northern Dynasties	北魏 Northern Wei Dynasty	386 - 534
		东魏 Eastern Wei Dynasty 北齐 Northern Qi Dynasty	534 - 550 550 - 577
		西魏 Western Wei Dynasty 北周 Northern Zhou Dynasty	535 - 556 557 - 581

187

隋 Sui Dynasty		581 - 618
唐 Tang Dynasty		618 - 907
五代十国 Five Dynasties and Ten States	后梁 Later Liang Dynasty	907 - 923
	后唐 Later Tang Dynasty	923 - 936
	后晋 Later Jin Dynasty	936 - 947
	后汉 Later Han Dynasty	947 - 950
	后周 Later Zhou Dynasty	951 - 960
	十国 Ten States**	902 - 979
宋 Song Dynasty	北宋 Northern Song Dynasty	960 - 1127
	南宋 Southern Song Dynasty	1127 - 1279
辽 Liao Dynasty		907 - 1125
西夏 Western Xia Dynasty		1038 - 1227
金 Jin Dynasty		1115 - 1234
元 Yuan Dynasty		1206 - 1368
明 Ming Dynasty		1368 - 1644
清 Qing Dynasty		1616 - 1911
中华民国 Republic of China		1912 - 1949

中华人民共和国1949年10月1日成立
People's Republic of China, founded on October 1, 1949

*"十六国"指东晋时期在我国北方等地建立的十六个地方割据政权，包括：汉（前赵）、成（成汉）、前凉、后赵（魏）、前燕、前秦、后燕、后秦、西秦、后凉、南凉、南燕、西凉、北凉、北燕、夏。
The "Sixteen States" refers to a series of local regimes established in the northern area and other regions of China during the Eastern Jin Dynasty, including Han (Former Zhao), Cheng (Cheng Han), Former Liang, Later Zhao (Wei), Former Yan, Former Qin, Later Yan, Later Qin, Western Qin, Later Liang, Southern Liang, Southern Yan, Western Liang, Northern Liang, Northern Yan, and Xia.

**"十国"指五代时期先后存在的十个地方割据政权，包括：吴、前蜀、吴越、楚、闽、南汉、荆南（南平）、后蜀、南唐、北汉。
The "Ten States" refers to the ten local regimes established during the Five Dynasties period, including Wu, Former Shu, Wuyue, Chu, Min, Southern Han, Jingnan (also Nanping), Later Shu, Southern Tang, and Northern Han.